Computacenter
Services & Solutions

NetApp®
Go further, faster

COMPUTACENTER AND NETAPP ARE PROUD
TO SUPPORT THE SOLDIERING ON TRUST
WHO ARE RECOGNISING LIFETIME
ACHIEVEMENTS IN RESPECT OF THE
BOMBER COMMAND MEMORIAL FUND

SOLDIERING ON AWARDS, THE WALDORF ASTORIA
SYON PARK, LONDON, 25 MARCH 2012

FIGHTING HIGH

WORLD WAR TWO – AIR BATTLE EUROPE

VOLUME ONE

Published in 2009 by Fighting High Ltd,
23 Hitchin Road, Stotfold, Hitchin, Herts, SG5 4HP.
United Kingdom. www.fightinghigh.com

British Library Cataloguing-in-Publication data.
A CIP record for this title is available from the British
Library below the copyright author listing on the title
page verso.

ISBN 978-0-9562696-0-7

Designed by Michael Lindley www.truthstudio.co.uk
Aircraft illustrations by Pete West.
Printed and bound in Malta by Progress Press.
Front cover illustration by Steve Teasdale.

FIGHTING HIGH

WORLD WAR TWO – AIR BATTLE EUROPE

VOLUME ONE

COMPILED AND EDITED BY

STEVE DARLOW

CONTENTS

24

32

40

WHILST RESEARCHING THE EXTRAORDINARY history of the Royal Air Force, the United States Army Air Force, and other Allied air forces in World War Two I managed to accumulate a wealth of first hand primary accounts concerning the European air battles. It is with pleasure that I present some of these here in this first volume of a new *Fighting High* series. (There is plenty more already in the archive for future volumes.) Compiling this volume of *Fighting High* gives us the chance to make these stories available to anyone with the desire to learn of the commitment, skill, and sacrifice of a generation of young men and women, whose fight must not be forgotten. Our focus has been to bring into public awareness the efforts of the men and women who fought against an aggressor hell-bent on imposing dictatorial rule and fascist tyranny on Europe.

Fighting High — World War Two — Air Battle Europe tells the story of the warriors of the air who fought in the aerial front line. The majority of the material in *Fighting High* has never been published in print before. In this series we are keen to promote the research and writing of new accounts of the air war. This series is about the human experience. We aim to make public the stories of those involved. It has often been difficult to get the veterans to open up. Some are fearful of 'shooting a line' and others have simply decided, until now, to keep it all in the past. When the war was over they had careers to develop and families to bring up. On many occasions family members have been unaware of what their husbands, fathers, or uncles actually went through. Fortunately our persuasive powers have worked enabling, us to record their remarkable stories. And we have not forgotten those unable to tell their story. The families of airmen lost during the war have given us access to relative's archives: logbooks, photographs, letters, and official documents.

The content of this book, as with future volumes, is based around certain core themes.

Veteran recollections – graphic first-hand accounts from those involved in the air campaigns.

Combat reports – notable encounters transporting the reader into the heat of a specific air battle.

Where the airmen lie – reflections at the final resting place of those who made the ultimate sacrifice, and their stories.

The air battle now – the present-day legacy of the battle: abandoned airfields, crash sites, memorials, artefacts, and warbirds.

In addition to the above there are a few Special Features, and in Volume One we are pleased to include pieces from noteworthy guest authors Robin J. Brooks, Lowell Getz, and Julian Evan-Hart.

This first volume of *Fighting High — World War Two — Air Battle Europe* sets the tone for future publications. In the following pages you will be able to read of the extraordinary exploits of a Beaufighter crew over the Mediterranean; an act of respect between two opposing fighter pilots over Sicily; the astonishing instinctive bravery of an airman hauling his injured colleague clear of a wrecked aircraft moments before the bombs explode; the sacrifice of two distinguished fighter pilots in the struggle to break out from the Normandy beaches; and a bomber pilots' helplessness as his aircraft breaks up around him and he falls to earth partially conscious.

It has been a real pleasure to travel around Europe researching the articles for this book, and a fascinating experience to sit down with the veterans and hear their tales. I hope you find the anecdotes and accounts in this and future publications similarly fascinating. Just by reading them you are keeping the memory alive. The 'Knights of the Air' are sadly, but inevitably, diminishing in numbers. It is truly an honour and privilege to present their stories, informing us today, and future generations, of their courage, bravery, heroism, and commitment whilst 'fighting high', ensuring the preservation of our liberties and freedoms.

Steve Darlow
August 2009

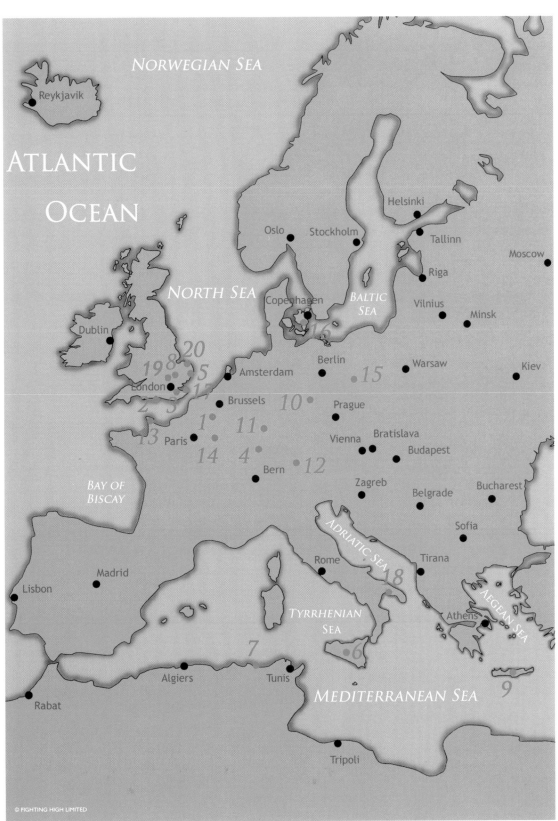

MCLEOD FAMILY

A Blenheim Boy
and the Battle of France

The British air forces were subjected to hard and costly lessons during the Battle of France in 1940. The commitment to defend their Allies against German aggression forced the British Government to honour a substantial deployment of men and materiel across the English Channel. All air forces fighting during the time of the Blitzkrieg suffered considerable attrition. Some aircraft were exposed as simply not being up to the task. **Donald McLeod**, one of the airmen who flew during the Battle of France, provides his opinion of the preparations for war, and his personal experience of adding to the loss statistics of the British air forces.

Donald McLeod followed not only in his father's footsteps, but also his grandfather's, when he signed up for military service in 1939, although Donald would face the enemy above ground level. Donald's father Percy 'joined a fighting regiment, just before one of the bloodiest wars in the history of the British Army' and his grandfather fought in the Boer War.

Donald, born on 16 September 1921, began work in the Post Office at the age of 16: 'I enjoyed the work very much, carrying out wiring and gaining experience in the battery room.' Whilst living in digs in Kensal Rise, London, Donald became aware of the Royal Air Force.

My landlady was a very fat Welsh woman and one of her sons, who was mad keen on aeroplanes, drew my attention to an advertisement in one of the daily papers, 'Join the RAF as a Direct Entry Sergeant Observer and fly'. Well the fat lady's son applied to join and I too was fired by the wording of this advertisement, flying around instead of working in the heat of a telephone exchange.

I applied and after an interview at the Air Ministry and a medical exam I was selected and told to report to St George's College in Northampton. I had no family to advise me, and it

seemed a good move to join the RAF. The older men in the telephone exchange thought I was crazy. "There is a war coming soon" they said "and you'll be dead in a month." I went to say goodbye to the boss. He wished me well and, shaking his head, hoped I would come back. He gave me the distinct impression that he entertained some doubt about my possible return.

To lads of seventeen and a half, the thought of war hardly entered our heads. If it came then this would add extra excitement. I wonder what would have happened to me had I stayed in London, faced the Blitz and not joined the RAF. Looking back I see quite clearly that the government knew damn well the war was coming against Germany and that maniac Hitler. Our government were recruiting too late and we were very badly under armed when war eventually came.

Donald reported to St George's College on 10 July 1939, one of approximately 60 raw recruits.

I think I was the youngest at two months short of eighteen, with some as old as twenty-five. I lost touch with the friends I made on the course. Most of them were killed in the first few months of the war.

The course at Northampton was to train us as navigators

and we were taught by ex-mariners. We were shown how to navigate by dead reckoning; finding the track of an aircraft and path along the ground by estimating the wind speed and direction, then setting a course to fly and calculating the estimated time of arrival at the target. There were so many probables that this method was prone to errors. There is a link between sea and air navigation, in that ships need to take account of tides and sea currents which act on the ships in a way similar to the effect of the wind on an aircraft. But there the similarity ends. A ship's average speed is about 10 knots, an aircraft flies at least ten times that speed. However, there was no one else to teach us, so we were stuck with ex-mariners. We put the classroom theory into practice on navigation training flights from the local airfield at Sywell; two trainees to each aircraft — Avro Ansons. The pilots were civilians and, if I remember rightly, they were not particularly interested in our progress in the air. We started off with short local flights and gradually these were increased to longer and longer flights until one day being told after take-off to prepare a course to Leuchars in Scotland. I had never flown so far from base before.

At the end of the course, which lasted three months, we took the examinations and were assessed on our abilities in the air. One or two chaps failed, and perhaps they were the lucky ones.

War was declared against Germany when Donald was midway through his course. Having passed the exams and 'been given a certificate to say that we were now competent navigators', Donald and his colleagues were posted to the next stage of their training.

We were sworn in officially to the RAF, issued with uniforms, and given the rank of Leading Aircraftmen. Half the course was sent to the bombing and gunnery course at Aldergrove, Northern Ireland and the other half to a bombing and gunnery course at Stormy Down, near Porthcawl, South Wales. This split into two was purely arbitrary and was based on alphabetical order of names, I was in the second batch M to Z. At Stormy we practised bombing over the bombing range in Cardigan Bay. At Aldergrove they used the Belfast Loch.

Donald's bombing practice was carried out in the single-engined light bomber, the Fairey Battle, which did not meet with his approval.

The Battle was the most awkward machine ever invented. The pilot sat in the front and the navigator lay in the belly of the aircraft. The air gunner would then pull his seat over the navigator and virtually be sitting on top of him. The navigator, lying prone, opened a hatch in the aircraft belly and navigated and bombed from this position. With the hatch open the exhaust from the engine came through into the navigator position. It was necessary to wear goggles and after landing the poor navigator looked like a pretend pilot in a Hollywood film.

For air firing we used very old Westland Wallaces and Wapatis, biplanes with open cockpits. A wire from the floor of the aircraft was attached to your parachute harness, called a monkey harness, which stopped you from falling out. We fired at drogues towed by other aircraft. Not a pleasant job for the pilots of these aircraft, with trainee gunners shooting live ammunition. We also practised firing from Whitley and Harrow bombers; lumbering old twin-engine aircraft, with a turret at each end. With a pupil in each turret, one would have red-tipped ammunition, so that when the drogue was released over the airfield, the number of bullet holes could be

counted and a score given by distinguishing the coloured holes from the plain ones.

After we qualified as bomb aimers and gunners we were deemed to be fit for war and sent to our operational training unit. I was posted with about 15 other chaps to *Andover* on Salisbury Plain where we were given our sergeant stripes and our wing, the famous flying 'O'. It is worth making clear that we new navigators were new to the RAF. From now on it was all experimental warfare as far as we were concerned. The brevet, the flying 'O', was issued to 'Observers' in the First World War. This wing was given to us and we too were called 'Observers'. Our job was to navigate the aircraft to the target, drop the bombs and fire the gun (if there was one to fire). Later on in the war the job was split into three separate parts, a navigator, a bomb aimer, and an air gunner, and each were given their own distinctive wing, worn above the left-hand breast pocket. We old navigators were rightly proud to wear our flying 'O' which distinguished us as from the old school.

It was at *Andover* that we were 'crewed up'; a pilot was given his own navigator and air gunner. My pilot, Michael Lovell, just 21, was from Jersey. Our air gunner's surname was Kenneth, I do not remember his Christian name. This completed the crew of our new Blenheim aircraft, a Mark IV. For some time we did a number of cross-country flights before being sent to France in the New Year of 1940.

Donald was posted to No. 53 Squadron at Poix, France. Without permanent billets Donald, with other navigators, found himself living above a local café.

We slept on straw palliasses in the loft, with no washing facilities except a cold-water pump in the yard. The weather was appalling: heavy snow falls all through the winter. When we were flying we were taken to the grass airfield at Croixrault, no concrete runway in those days, about two miles from the village of Poix. I remember how primitive and so very poor the whole place seemed. This was an agricultural area and the standard of living of the peasants was very poor. We were paid in French money and I remember that nobody in the village could change the thousand franc note with which we were paid. This note was riches indeed to the villagers.

After some time, having got absolutely fed up with sleeping on straw, most of us found civilian digs with French families. I can't remember the name of the old lady I stayed with, but

"We slept on straw palliasses in the loft, with no washing facilities except a cold-water pump in the yard"

I do remember I was able to sleep in an enormous feather bed for which I paid the princely sum of about two shillings and sixpence a week, half a crown in old money.

On the airfield, which we shared with No. 59 Squadron, we were divided into flights dispersed around the airfield as a precaution against air attack. We flew quite a lot on practice cross-countries and made sorties from our advanced airfield at Metz. I remember one extremely eventful trip when our crew were detailed to fly to Metz with a spare crew to bring back a Blenheim that had been repaired. We flew over the town of Lyon and were surprised to see it on fire. On arriving at Metz we were surrounded by excited ground crew saying they had just been bombed. An air raid was sounded and we all trouped into an enormous underground shelter. The airfield was bombed again, the grass field was pitted with bomb holes and the aircraft we had come to collect was badly damaged.

Metz was where the Germans developed the use of airships in the First World War. I can remember that the aircraft we had come to fetch was in one of the very large airship hangers. The side had been blown away and this aircraft was no longer in a fit condition to fly. After having lunch we made ready to return to base at Poix. Unfortunately on take-off we went down one of the bomb holes and our own aircraft was damaged beyond repair. We swivelled round with the propellers dug into the ground. Luckily the aircraft did not catch fire so we were able to scramble out. There was nothing we could do but return by train to Poix, some hundreds of miles. We decided to take the train to Paris, stay the night there and return to Poix the next day. When we arrived at the railway station it was packed with French and Belgium refugees fleeing from the advancing German army. No one had told us that the Germans had broken through the frontiers that very day and were making rapid progress into France. There was absolute chaos. The station was overflowing with refugees. We were lucky to get on a train with standing room only and it took many hours to reach Paris, arriving late that night. I slept in a hotel and I had not been asleep very long before we were all ordered out and directed down into the Metro in the Place de la Concord. We felt a little conspicuous in our flying gear. I am sure we enjoyed the attention, but would never have admitted it.

Next morning we were able to get a train to Amiens and then eventually to Poix. On returning we learnt that the squadron had been active against the advancing Germans and had carried out a number of raids reconnoitring the area towards the Albert Canal. We were alarmed when told that a number of our aircrews had been shot down or had returned badly shot up, with casualties.

The German Army opened their offensive into Holland, Belgium and Luxembourg at first light on 10 May 1940. Simultaneously the Luftwaffe bombed enemy airfields and communications, including those in France. Over the next few days the attrition rates, for both sides, were high. Notably weaknesses were exposed in the aircraft of the British air forces operational in France. The Battle and Blenheim squadrons suffered unsustainable loss rates. Historians, with the benefit of hindsight, claim that many operations flown by the Battle and Blenheim crews were suicidal. Donald McLeod's experience was a case in point, with No. 53 Squadron, part of 5 (Reconnaissance) Wing with the RAF Component, British Expeditionary Force.

The Germans had an enormous advantage at this time; they had superior air cover using their Messerschmitt 109s to do this job. There were hundreds of them saturating and covering the German advance. They were well trained and their aircraft were superior in speed and fire power. Some of the 109s fired explosive cannon shells, standing off at 1,000 yards. Our feeble reply was from one gun in the turret of the Blenheim, which fired .303 ammunition. Not a patch on the cannon fire of the Messerschmitt. Our squadron valiantly carried on

MONSIEUR DELFORGE

against these superior odds, losing one aircraft after another. I have heard reports that the German airmen said it was like duck shooting, it was so easy.

On 16 May 1940 our crew were ordered to patrol the region of the Albert Canal up to the town of Maastricht for two hours and then we would be relieved. We were to have two Hurricanes to accompany us. On the evening of 15 May we flew up to our new advanced airfield at Vitry-en-Artois; the original one at Metz had quickly been overrun by the advancing German army. We were to be in the air by dawn of 16 May and proceed to our rendezvous with the Hurricanes. We were told by the briefing officer, a Major in the army, that if we flew at 3,700 feet we would be too low to be troubled by heavy anti-aircraft fire and too high for small-arms fire. What a bloody idiot he was. I learnt much later that he got this advice out of an army manual. He knew nothing of aerial warfare, the plonker!!! Well we duly met our supporting Hurricanes at 0515, and went on our merry way. The front line was much more advanced than we had been told and within minutes we were meeting an enormous barrage of anti-aircraft fire. We were flying directly into the rising sun and we were blinded and unable to see very far in front of us. The rule was always approach the Hun from the sun, i.e. with the sun behind you. Come out of the sun if possible. We were in exactly the wrong position. The anti-aircraft fire stopped, a sure sign that enemy fighters were about. Suddenly there were enemy fighters everywhere; they were stacked up in layers. Our valiant Hurricanes, instead of protecting us, engaged the enemy planes. What happened to them I do not know, they must have been shot down. As I have said, our armament was one fixed gun firing forward in the leading edge of the aircraft and one gun firing from the rear turret. This gun was a Vickers gas-operated gun synchronised with its sights at 250 yards; it fired .303 bullets which if they ever reached the enemy aircraft would have done no damage at all. It would have been like throwing peas at them. I, the navigator, had no gun at all and had to sit there and hope for the best. The Me109s just stayed out of range and fired explosive cannon shell into us. Suddenly there was an almighty bang. I was hit in the head by shrapnel, through the leg and through the shoulder. My pilot was looking dazed at the controls as he too had been hit down his right side, in fact I could see a wound through his chin. By this time we had descended to 50 feet trying to shake off the enemy plane. How my pilot ever got the aircraft down on the

ground I shall never know. I remember moving back and helping him to throttle the engines back, for he seemed to be hit in his hand and was unable to slow the engines down. Somehow we belly flopped in a ploughed field with the wheels up. We came to a grinding halt and all was suddenly quiet. Our air gunner had somehow managed to avoid being badly hit, although I think he lost a finger, but apart from that he was unharmed. We managed to get the pilot out, who by this time was unconscious. We gave him a shot of morphine, which we carried for such emergencies, and he seemed to be a little more comfortable. I lay on the wing covered in blood. After some time, I have no knowledge of how long it was, two women came to our aid. They tried to bandage my head and one of the women put a pillow under the pilot's head; I also remember that we were wrapped in blankets. Eventually a car arrived and took us to a clinic in the nearest town of Péruwelz on the France – Belgium border. The place where we had crashed was near a very small village called Wadelincourt. In the clinic we were given some aid; unfortunately there were no doctors there.

As the German advance continued, efforts were made to evacuate Donald from the area, but there is little he can remember, owing to his injuries and the effects of pain killers.

I remember being put on a stretcher and being carried in some sort of vehicle from the ploughed field. I later found out that Monsieur Rene Husson, who was in charge of a local 'home guard', sent a car to take me to the clinic. This he was not authorised to do, but by doing so he saved my life. How I got eventually to a French hospital on the French coast I do not know. What I do know is that a hospital ship that was taking wounded soldiers on board was bombed by the Germans, with many lives lost.

We were being shelled by the advancing Germans and the hospital was told to evacuate. I still had shrapnel in my head and leg but I was given a shot of something and told to walk, if

MONSIEUR DELFORGE

possible, to the railway station. I must have fainted on the way and the next thing I remember was being on a train with some soldiers but again, I do not know what happened next. I woke up in a soft bed, in a room by myself with a nurse at my side. I could not make myself understood as this was, I learnt later, a casualty clearing station for the French wounded at the Grand Hotel at Deauville on the French coast. I do not know how long I was in this hospital hotel but they were very kind to me. I was called 'l'enfant' as they thought I was so young.

I had an operation on my head to remove the shrapnel and had a piece of skull removed, which left a hole in my head. I thought, later, that I would need to have a plate fitted. I spoke no French and they spoke no English. The surgeon was a French army doctor. I distinctly remember he was a little drunk when

he removed the stitches from my head. But he must have been a very good surgeon for I have had little trouble since then, although it did leave me with nervous problems. I was shell shocked and the effects remain after nearly sixty years. However, apart from having the inconvenience of having a hole in my nut, I must be thankful that I do not suffer more from my wounds. That surgeon saved my life. I learnt later that he and his wife were tortured and killed by the Gestapo, accused of being members of the Resistance.

Above: Donald, on left, during his recuperation in the UK.

Top right: A Monsieur Ledru presenting Donald in 1989 with parts of the Blenheim, recovered and hidden under a rabbit hutch throughout the war.

Centre right: During his 1989 visit to Belgium, Donald is presented to one of the ladies (in the white cardigan) who assisted him that fateful morning 49 years ago.

Bottom right: Donald at the scene of the crash of Blenheim L4860 PZ-W.

As the Germans approached the town a decision was made to move the hospital south. In the meantime the staff began moving patients into the basement because of shelling. But for Donald, 'I had no wish to be sent further into France.' He was then subject to 'an incredible stroke of luck' when an English lorry stopped outside the hospital, en route to evacuation at Cherbourg, and the matron informed two soldiers that they were looking after an Englishman. 'These two soldiers, looked after me as though I was a child.'

I was on a stretcher and they gave me food and water and tried to make me as comfortable as possible. We were unable to get to Cherbourg in one journey and stayed the night in Caen. The next day we went to Cherbourg and I was put on one of the

last boats to reach England. It probably sounds corny but the sight of the white cliffs of Dover was a sight I shall always remember. Who these soldiers were I do not know to this day but they saved my life. I was taken off the boat and we were met by crowds of people who handed out goodies. I had no idea what was happening, which was quite normal, nobody told you anything. In fact you gave up asking and just let things happen.

Donald spent the next few days on a hospital train, finally ending up at the Stirlingshire and District Mental Hospital.

The mental patients had been sent somewhere else and this was now a full-blown military hospital, run on military lines. Having your hands out of the bed as the matron passed by was a sin. I was the only RAF patient in the hospital, possibly because most of the airmen who were wounded were in enemy countries. I stayed in the Stirlingshire hospital until I was fit enough to walk.

For some reason the wound on my head would not heal. I was sent to the Edinburgh Royal Infirmary and came under the care of Professor Norman Dott, one of the most eminent brain specialists of his day. There was talk of fitting a metal plate to the hole in my head but Professor Dott decided that the skull would grow a reasonably hard protective layer. So thanks to him it was never fitted.

I left Edinburgh with my wounds mended but had a measure of shell shock or whatever they called it in those days. The slightest noise or bang and I would leap into the air. With typical service compassion they sent me to convalesce in London during the Blitz.

I was sent for a day to an RAF Medical Centre at Farnborough, where I was put into a decompression chamber which simulated gradually flying at increased heights. I suppose this was to check on the effect the head wound had on my ability to stand different air pressures. Finally I was given a medical category of limited flying.

Donald's operational days were over, although he still had important duties to fulfil. His future with the Royal Air Force was as a navigational instructor, taking up the offer of passing on his knowledge in Canada. But that's another story. ∎

Donald McLeod sadly passed away early in 2008. My thanks to his wife Ruth, and their children Chris, Gill, and Fiona, for their help with this article.

Left: The parts of Blenheim L4860 PZ-W given to Donald when he returned to Belgium in 1989.
Top: Aero-engine starter. Centre: Aero magneto. Bottom: Engine speed indicator.

Below: Donald McLeod in Belgium.

GORDON MITCHELL
ONE OF THE FEW

There are many churchyards the length and breadth of the United Kingdom that host the final resting place of Royal Air Force airmen. For many, but by no means all, their graves are marked with the distinctive, simple, outline of a white headstone, provided by that extraordinary organisation – the Commonwealth War Graves Commission. To the east of Willian (All Saints) Church, near Letchworth, Hertfordshire, England, is one such headstone marking the grave of one of the Battle of Britain's 'Few'.

Right: The final resting place of Gordon Mitchell – All Saints churchyard, Willian, Hertfordshire.

GORDON THOMAS MANNERS MITCHELL

Rank Pilot Officer
Unit 609 Squadron
Date of Death 11/07/1940
Service No. 90484
Son of Thomas Robert
and Sarah Agnes Mitchell,
of Letchworth. BA Hons.
(Cantab)
Place of Burial
Willian (All Saints) churchyard,
Willian, near Letchworth,
Hertfordshire

Background

Gordon Mitchell was born on 24 September 1910, in Ceylon. He carried out his education at Caldicott School, Hitchin, then Leys School, Cambridge, and on to Queens' College, studying Law and Economics. Gordon was a noted sportsman, a member of the College's tennis team, and a Cambridge Blue and Scottish International at Hockey. He also developed a keenness and aptitude for flying, becoming a member of the University Air Squadron in the early 1930s. In 1933 Gordon travelled abroad to work in Sarawak, and a few years later returned to England to continue his career.

Gordon's desire to fly was met by the Auxiliary Air Force and he obtained a commission with No. 609

'West Riding' Squadron in November 1938. As war loomed, flying became his full-time occupation and he developed his flying skills at 6 FTS, Little Rissington from October 1939. Gordon then rejoined No. 609 Squadron at Northolt in May 1940.

Gordon got to grips flying Spitfires and saw considerable action with the squadron over Dunkirk. With the remnants of the British Expeditionary Force finally evacuated, Hitler and the Luftwaffe delayed the assault on England, allowing the RAF, in particular, to regroup and prepare.

Into July 1940 and the Luftwaffe began to test the British defences, attacking seaborne convoys steaming along the south and east coasts. They carried vital resources and had to be protected, and many a fighter pilot found himself patrolling in defence of such convoys. On 4 July No. 609 Squadron received orders to move to Middle Wallop. The Battle of Britain is now deemed to have officially opened on 10 July with raids on convoys off North Foreland and Dover, during which 13 German aircraft and 6 RAF fighters fell. Early the next day it appeared that the Luftwaffe were preparing for another scrap over the sea, in which 'Mitch' and his squadron colleagues would seek to oppose them.

The fateful day

At 0730 hours on the morning of 11 July 1940 radar picked up a contact in the direction of Portland, on the south coast of England. Luftlotte 3 aircraft, flying from the Cherbourg peninsula, had set out to attack a shipping convoy in the Lyme Bay area. At dawn No. 609 Squadron had sent some of its Spitfires from Middle Wallop to Warmwell. The call came through to take to the air and patrol off Portland, and at 0750 hours five Spitfires flown by Philip 'Pip' Barran,

Gordon Mitchell, Jarvis Blayney, Bernard Little, and John Curchin were airborne. Gordon was flying L1095.

Fifteen miles south of Portland the No. 609 Squadron pilots came into contact with the enemy. Pip Barran sighted some Junker 87s in line astern gliding in to strike at a ship and he ordered his colleagues to turn and position themselves between the sun and the bombers. Barran then led Blue Section, three aircraft, in line astern into the attack, whilst Green section, two aircraft weaving behind, acted as a rear guard. But it seems as if they had fallen into a trap.

As the attacking Spitfires homed in, Blayney, flying as Blue 3, had his attention grabbed by bullets fizzing past his windscreen. He had little choice but to abandon the attack on the Stukas, and take evasive action, broadcasting a warning to his colleagues. Having carried out a sharp turn he found himself free of danger. Blayney scanned the sky, sighting a Ju87 at 1,500 feet. He seized his chance, opening fire at 200 yards,

Left: Pre-war picture of Gordon Mitchell.

closing to 50 yards, his 2–3 second burst hitting home and the Ju87 zigzagging into the sea.

With no further enemy aircraft in sight Blayney remained above the bombed ship but then he caught sight of Blue 1, Pip Barran, making for the English coast, fire and smoke belching

Right: At 0750 hours five pilots of 609 Squadron take to the air. Only three return.

Bernard Little, suddenly found himself amidst a swarm of Me109s, also noticing Blue Section under attack. Little threw his aircraft around the sky, and then found himself mixing it with some Ju87s. As one of the Stukas dived toward the sea Little unleashed a quick burst of metal which struck

Me109s on his tail. He sent his Spitfire into evasive manoeuvres and by the time he had lost them the Ju87s were nowhere in sight. Curchin saw some enemy fighters 10 miles away, and then a pilot, undoubtedly Pip Barran, baling out from a burning Spitfire.

Curchin, Blayney, and Little returned

from his Spitfire. Blayney turned and followed until he saw Barran's engine stop a few miles south of Portland Bill, at which point Barran baled out, floating down into the sea. He was later picked up by the Navy, but died owing to the severity of his burns.

Meanwhile, the pilots in Green section, to the rear, were also flying and fighting for their lives. Green 1,

Right: Per Adua Ad Astra... Thy Will Be Done.

home. The No. 609 Squadron pilot had no time to watch and see if it hit the water, he was flying for his life and such a lapse would have been fatal, but he later reported that his adversary was falling, inverted, with small pieces breaking away.

In the melee Green 2, John Curchin, had also managed to get behind a Ju87, but he then found he had two

to tell of the fight. News of Barran's death soon came through. But what of Gordon? He had been part of Blue Section but had failed to return, and the No. 609 Squadron Intelligence Officer could get little information from the other pilots. Gordon was recorded as missing and for a few days no news came through as to his fate. Eventually his death was reported – his body

having washed ashore at Newport on the Isle of Wight. (Mitch had been shot down by Oberleutnant Dobislav of III/JG27 flying a Messerschmitt Bf 109E). Gordon Mitchell's funeral was held on 25 July 1940.

No. 609 Squadron's experience on the morning of 11 July formed part of Fighter Command's steep learning curve in the early days of the Battle of Britain. The No. 609 Squadron diarist pulled no punches in recording his feelings on the tactics used.

The utter futility of sending a very small section of fighters to cope with the intense enemy activity in the Portland area is bitterly resented by the pilots. The fact that they have so often been sent off to make an interception — as a Section, or possibly a Flight — only to find themselves hopelessly outnumbered by enemy fighters acting as guard to the bombers, is discouraging because the British fighter then finds himself unable to do his job of destroying the bombers, and is compelled to fight a defensive action. The situation is keenly felt by this Squadron, whose 'score' of enemy aircraft is in too close a ration to its own losses. It is felt that we happen to have been particularly unlucky in that both at Dunkirk and at Portland our contacts with the enemy have taken place when the numerical odds were rather too unreasonable.

One member of the squadron, in particular, also 'keenly felt' Gordon Mitchell's loss. In his book *Spitfire Pilot* No. 609 Squadron pilot David Crook DFC recorded his feelings.

Gordon's death in particular made a deep impression on me, because I knew him much better than I knew Pip. We were at school together, and he, Michael, and I had spent the whole war together, and were so accustomed to being in each other's company that I could not then (and still cannot now) get used to the idea that we should not see Gordon again or spend any more of our gay evenings together or rag him about the moustache of which he was so proud.

He was a delightful person, a very amusing and charming companion and one of the most generous people I ever knew, both as regards material matters and, more important still, in his outlook and views.

He was also a brilliant athlete, a Cambridge Hockey Blue and Scots International. It always used to delight me to watch Gordon playing any game, whether hockey, tennis, or squash, because he played with such a natural ease and grace — the unmistakable sign of a first-class athlete.

He could not have wished to die in more gallant circumstances. ■

Left:
The Commonwealth War Graves Commission headstone memorialising Battle of Britain pilot Gordon Mitchell.

CHAPTER THREE

VIA ROBIN J. BROOKS

A True
Heroine

On 24 September 1940, a Royal Warrant announced the institution of a new decoration – the George Cross. Known as the 'Civilians' VC' it was to become the most coveted award for bravery. It was ordained that the persons eligible for the decoration of the Cross should be, amongst others,'persons of any rank in the Naval, Military or Air Forces of Our United Kingdom of Great Britain'. The first person to receive the George Cross was Daphne Joan Mary Pearson, a 'Fair Maid' of Kent who had enlisted in the Women's Auxiliary Air Force. **Robin J. Brooks** tells her story of courage and heroism.

Corporal Daphne Joan Mary Pearson was a member of No. 500 (County of Kent) Squadron, Royal Auxiliary Air Force which in 1940 was stationed at Detling, high up on the North Downs near Maidstone, Kent, England. Serving in the medical section, she had attended to many minor injuries but nothing was to prepare her for the night that an Avro Anson crashed with all its bombs aboard. Her prompt action undoubtedly saved the life of the pilot.

Operation Dundee

Detling was a Coastal Command base in No. 16 (General Reconnaissance) Group with its headquarters at Chatham. No. 500 Squadron was engaged on maritime reconnaissance flying the Avro Anson Mk 1. Additional

the explosion would have surely killed them both. Laying there for some minutes whilst further lesser explosions took place, Daphne tidied Bond as best as possible until the ambulance arrived. Only when she had assured herself that no more assistance could be given and that there was no hope of rescuing the navigator did she leave the scene. The total act had been done entirely without thought for her own safety.

Completely unawed by her heroic deed, she wrote to her mother in Cornwall saying that she had been involved in a 'little something'. "My name has been sent to the King," she said, "but I hope nothing will be done about it. When I read of the things our boys did at Dunkirk my little big seems nothing at all." The King, however had different thoughts on the act and courage of this brave woman.

"I congratulate you"
In June 1940, Daphne Pearson received her commission and the following month the *London Gazette* announced that Corporal (now Assistant Section Officer) Pearson had been awarded the medal that ranked next to the Victoria Cross, the Medal of the Military Division of the British Empire for Gallantry, the EGM. On a hot day in August she went to Buckingham Palace for the investiture and ended up fetching water and caring for all of the men who fainted in the extreme heat that August. Again in 1941 she went back to the Palace for the second investiture to exchange her Gallantry Medal for the George Cross. Lord Clarendon, the Lord Chamberlain, read from the official account of how Section Officer Pearson had saved the life of a seriously injured pilot of a crashed aircraft. The King told her "You are the first woman to win the George Cross. I congratulate you."

Daphne's interest in flying began in her teens with regular visits to Ramsgate Airport. She took a series of flying lessons and was about to take her civil pilot's licence when the war intervened. Joining the 19th ATS Company attached to the Royal West Kent Regiment, she was one of 15 girls transferred to become the nucleus of the WAAF attached to No. 500 Squadron at Detling. When told women were not permitted to fly in wartime, she was offered a post in the medical section, becoming the first female medical orderly in the squadron.

Reunion
Leaving Detling in 1941 she served at several Bomber Command stations until the end of the war. Although moving to Australia shortly after, she regularly attended the VC and GC reunions held in the UK each year and it was at one such reunion that a telephone call united her with the family of Pilot Officer David Bond.

Although having not seen David Bond since that fateful night, she had often wondered what had become of him. Fifty-five years later she was to find out when the VC/GC reunion in May 1995, and the fact that only nine holders of either award were present, was reported in the national press. By chance David Bond's family saw the report and immediately tracked Daphne down. Although their father had died in 1977, he had survived the war and went on to found what was to become Bond Helicopters, one of the world's largest civilian helicopter companies.

Having managed to contact Daphne at the RAF Club in Piccadilly shortly after the reunion, the family arranged for

Left: Daphne is united with Stephen and Geoffrey Bond, sons of the father she saved.

her and her companion, Audrey Jarvis, to fly to Aberdeen, the headquarters of the company. Upon arrival the couple took their first helicopter flight and were taken to lunch at Raemoir House Hotel, Banchory in Royal Deeside. It was here that the family got the chance to thank Daphne personally for saving their father's life. Stephen Bond, now the company managing director, said that it was a family business and that had it not been for Daphne's heroic act, Bond Helicopters may never have been. He further added that the family had waited 55 years to thank her in person. Daphne was equally delighted to meet them saying that it was difficult in wartime to keep track of people. Although she had received a letter from an aunt of David Bond, she never saw him again once he was sent to hospital.

Sadly Daphne died on 25 July 2000 in Melbourne. She was a true heroine of her time and it was fitting that in her latter years she would meet what she described as a 'whole new family'. ∎

Bomber Command veteran Wing Commander Richard Pinkham DFC survived two tours of operations in the struggle against Germany. He was one of the other 'Few' during the Battle of Britain, having arrived at No. 77 Squadron on 30 June 1940. Over the course of those momentous summer months Richard was regularly over Germany, or bombing Hitler's invasion barges in the Channel ports. And when the Luftwaffe switched to the night Blitz of British cities, Richard and his Bomber Command colleagues took the fight back to the Reich. There was much still to be learnt, as Richard's recollections of one particular night show.

Not Likely to Forget

RICHARD PINKHAM

Richard Pinkham's first operational tour took place in the days before there were Pathfinders to mark the way and locate targets and before the introduction of 'bomber streams' to concentrate attacks. And the tools of the trade, such as the Armstrong Whitworth Whitley, now appear, in comparison to the latter-day four-engine heavy bombers, quite basic and rudimentary. But at the time they were all Bomber Command had with which to fight back.

We had to do the best we could with Whitley Vs with Merlin X engines. Great lumbering 'crates'. With full load, you needed all the take-off run you could get. She would get 'unstuck' at about 85 knots, and a normal cruising speed of about 135 knots. But they were built as solid as the rock of Gibraltar, and capable of taking a lot of punishment! But if you had engine failure, you'd no time to look around for a nice comfortable spot to make a forced landing. The training we had carrying out emergency landings on Tiger Moths, had very little relevance for these flying coffins. Still, we should not disparage the old 'crates' as they stood me in good stead on a few occasions.

On 3 December 1940 Bomber Command sent out 20 aircraft to targets in Germany, with No. 77 Squadron's Pilot Officer Richard Pinkham at the controls of Whitley V P4299 'J'. Richard lifted his 'crate' at 1624 hours from the RAF Topcliffe runway, detailed to bomb the Mannheim central railway junction. He was nearing the end of his first tour and his account of this flight provides a good example of the nature of operational flying at that time, when the bomber offensive was in its infancy. Richard had flown on an operation to Hamburg on 16 November and then enjoyed some leave, 'much needed after four sorties in seven nights, all long flights'.

Battle of wits

This trip was one I was not likely to forget. There was a full moon and cloudless sky and at 12,000 feet, we felt naked and quite sure we could be seen by night fighters from miles away. Mannheim is about 300 miles from the Dutch coast and the route took us very near to some heavily defended areas. The total time over enemy territory would be about five hours, and as this was

RICHARD PINKHAM

one of the brightest nights, we had to be on a sharp look-out for fighters all the time.

There was a very strong tail-wind on the route out and to take full advantage we climbed to 14,000 feet with a wind speed of about eighty knots. We could always see the flashes of the heavy flak firing on the ground, so at that height a slight alteration of course would take you well clear of where the shells would burst. It would take several seconds for the shell to reach us after it had been fired and it became something of a battle of wits between the gunners on the ground and us. When the shells burst well away from us I just laughed and said, 'Missed again, you silly buggers!' We treated it very much as a game, the thought of them getting a lucky hit never occurred to me.

Missed!

The moon was still high, casting a bluish-grey pearly lustre over the ground below. It was a glorious night; there was something surrealistic about the scene. It was this experience which I enjoyed about night flying. We continued on a course keeping well to the south-west of Cologne and other heavily defended areas. There was a very strong westerly wind, with at least a 10 degree drift; we flew on a course of 140 degrees. There was no difficulty in finding the target area. Mannheim is situated at the confluence of the rivers Neckar and Rhein, a landmark which stood out in the moonlight. The target itself was not so easy to pick out. We wanted to make absolutely sure we were 'spot on' and not waste our bombs, so we

Above: Richard Pinkham at No. 3 Flying Training School, South Cerney, December 1939.

Main image left: Richard Pinkham standing third from the right at No. 77 Squadron.

Below: Entry from Richard Pinkham's logbook.

STEVE DARLOW

| WHITLEY V | T4226 | SELF | | CREW | BXC | MANNHEIM | TARGET LOCATED | 24 |
| WHITLEY V | T4299 | SELF | | CREW | | LOCAL FLYING, AIR TEST | | |

RICHARD PINKHAM

Above: No. 77
Squadron Whitley Vs.

'stooged' around for nearly an hour until we were certain we had identified the target. Even then after taking so much trouble to be sure, we made a good run-up to the target and missed! With the high wind the bomb aimer had possibly not allowed enough drift on his bomb sight. It was probably a near miss, but we were certainly not 'bang on'. Everything was in our favour, good visibility, and a good steady run-up to the target, but we missed. Up to then, everything had gone fine, and we set course for home.

Flying at 14,000 feet we had taken full advantage of the tail wind, but as this would be against us on the return flight I decided to descend to a level where the head wind would not be so strong. As we had not encountered any flak on the way out I considered there would be no risk, and came down to 3,000 feet. I had the second pilot in the front turret map reading, and he gave me frequent pin-points, and with the brilliant moon light it was easy enough to pick out rivers which gave me reassurance that we were right on track. We were aiming to cross the Dutch coast at the Schelde islands, which would have taken us well south of Rotterdam, but we were about 25 miles off track. I kept checking with the second pilot, and he assured me 'We're bang on track skipper'. Several times I checked with him and he seemed to be quite positive. A few more miles and we would be over the North Sea.

"I think I've been hit..."

Suddenly, without any warning, every searchlight in the area fastened on to us. There must have been at least fifty. Instantly, all the guns opened up with light flak and tracer. It was coming at us from all directions! The inevitable happened; we got a direct hit in the fuselage. I really thought we had had it. But blinded by the searchlights all I could do was to get my head down, push the stick hard forward and with nose well down, beat the hell out of it. This time Jerry was laughing at me. I thought that will teach me to have more respect for the Jerry gunners in future.

Somehow we were still flying under control, and there did not appear to have been any damage to engines or vital controls. I kept the nose down until we were out of danger and out over the sea. I called up each of the crew in turn, to find out if they were all right, but Paddy the rear gunner replied, "I'm all right skipper, I'm all right skipper", repeating everything strictly according to patter. "I think I've been hit skipper — I think I've been hit." Then, "I don't think it has penetrated far. I don't think it has penetrated far. I can't see any sign of blood. I can't see any sign of blood." Of course everyone could see the funny side of it, and roared with laughter. One could imagine poor Paddy bouncing up in his turret, feeling under his backside. "I don't think it has penetrated far", conjured

RICHARD PINKHAM

up images of blood gushing everywhere. I sent the wireless operator down to see him to see if he needed assistance; in the meantime I asked him if he could get out of his turret but he replied, "OK skipper, I'm all right!", again repeating it. But at least he did not sound distressed or in any agony. The W/Op came back, and reported that the fuselage was in a bit of a mess. As soon as we were clear of the Dutch coast, I handed over control to the second pilot, and went back to see for myself what damage had been done. A shell had burst in the fuselage, with holes everywhere. It looked like a colander. Still we were flying quite normal. I was astonished to find that the elevator control cables on the port side had been completely severed. Hopelessly I picked up the loose ends and contemplated the improbability of joining them, but as we did not carry cable spares, there was no hope of carrying out running repairs. Glancing at the port side I was relieved to see that the duplicate set of cables was intact. I was naturally very concerned for Paddy, but despite my entreaty for him to come out of his turret, he insisted on "sticking to his guns". He certainly did not appear to have been injured. The rest of the flight across the North Sea was uneventful. It was a beautiful night, with millions of bright stars, and the moon reflecting in the sea. This was the sort of experience for which I thoroughly enjoyed night flying.

Recalling the ordeal of being caught in the searchlights and sustaining a direct hit, seemed more like awakening from an all too realistic nightmare. We landed safely after being in the air for ten and a quarter hours, but very thankful to be back on 'terra firma'.

As soon as we landed, we examined Paddy's flying clothing, to find there were holes on both sides, which looked as if the shell splinter had passed right through his clothing. We piled into the dispersal truck, and lost no time getting back to the locker room to get Paddy's clothing off. Sure enough there were holes through his uniform trousers, but not a scratch on his skin. No wonder he thought, "I think I've been hit. I don't think it has penetrated far." ■

Above left: Squadron Leader Richard Pinkham DFC, September 1944, when serving with the 3rd Tactical Air Force, Comilla, Bengal.

Below left: Wing Commander Richard Pinkham DFC at the signing of *Special Op: Bomber* May 2008.

STEVE DARLOW

With Pleasure
Your Majesty

I suppose you could not really ask for a much more noteworthy spectator than your sovereign head of state. As luck would have it, on 27 January 1943, Pilot Officer Cecil 'Tommy' Cody, was able to perform for his King and Queen, and then tell them about his encounter over a cup of tea. Could it be any more 'English'?

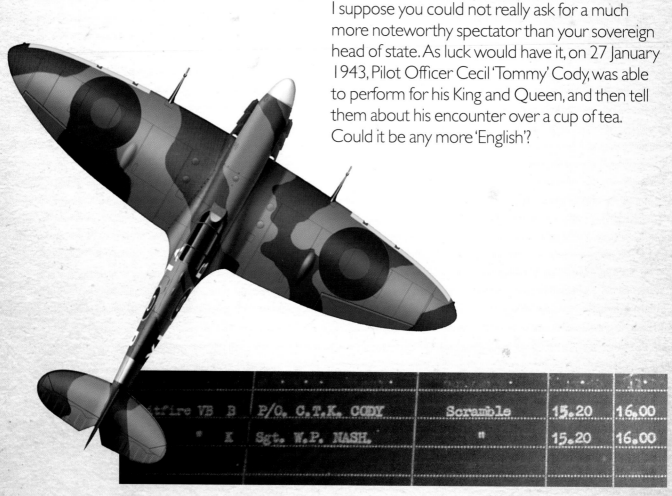

| tfire VB B | P/O. C.T.K. CODY | Scramble | 15.20 | 16.00 |
| " X | Sgt. W.P. NASH. | " | 15.20 | 16.00 |

On 27 January 1943 the No. 167 (Gold Coast) Squadron diarist recorded, 'Great News! The King and Queen are coming to Ludham tomorrow. It's certainly wonderful how things can be done in view of the visit, the mess is being re-painted.' And the following day the diarist maintained his enthusiastic tone. 'A real "Red Letter" day which should put 167 Squadron on the map once and for all. At 15.20 just as the King and Queen were due to arrive, there is a scramble and P/O "Tommy" Cody and Sgt Nash take off to investigate, find a Ju88, shoot it down into the sea off Yarmouth, all within 9 minutes. During this time

the King and Queen have arrived and while being introduced to the whole Squadron in "A" Flight dispersal the news comes through from Ops that a Ju88 had been shot down. Good Show Cody and that's right – "pick your time". Needless to say the King and Queen were thrilled and asked everyone all manner of questions, also asked that the pilots be sent up to them in the Mess as soon as they landed. A good many of the Squadron had tea in the Mess with the King and Queen and Cody and Nash were introduced to them, shooting the most colossal line (I expect) on how easy it is to shoot down the Hun.'

TOMMY CODY'S SPITFIRE VB ILLUSTRATION BY PETE WEST

COMBAT REPORT

FROM:	167 (Gold Coast) Squadron, Ludham
TO:	Headquarters, Fighter Command
DATE:	28 January 1943
AIRCRAFT:	2 Spitfires VB
TIME:	1529 hrs
POSITION:	4 miles S.E. of Yarmouth
CONDITIONS:	Visibility 2 miles; very hazy in patches. Cloud 10/10 at 1,000 ft
OUTCOME:	1 Ju88 destroyed

C.T.K. CODY VIA GRUB STREET

General report

2 L.R. Spitfires VB, 167 Squadron, P/O Cody and Sgt Nash, Red 1 and 2, were scrambled from Ludham 1520 hrs, to intercept Raid No. X 98, with instructions to vector 140 degrees at Angels 1. After a few minutes flying, the Section were told to patrol coast off Yarmouth and to look out for bogey. Red 1 during this time saw two Venturas flying West at 0 feet. As the Section turned South, Red 2 saw an aircraft in the haze 1000 yards to Port, which was later identified as a Ju88 flying at 100 feet in a westerly direction. The e/a on seeing Red Section pulled up to 400-500 feet opening fire with machine gun from top turret, and turned to the South, when Red 1 got in a 3-4 seconds burst of c and m.g. from 300 yards closing to 150 yards, seeing strikes along the fuselage and Port wing on fire between engine and fuselage. E/A then started to disintegrate in the air, did a stall turn to Port, and went into the sea, 4 miles S.E. of Yarmouth, 1 (one) of the crew baling out. E/A was later seen to be burning on the sea for some considerable time. Red Section continued the patrol and returned to base at 1600 hrs. Cine-gun carried and exposed.

P/O Cody claims Ju88 destroyed*.

Armament report

P/Cody

20 m.m. Ball	17 rounds	.303 A.P.	200 rounds
20 m.m. H.E./I	16 rounds	.303 Incendiary MkVIIx	200 rounds

Stoppages
Port cannon. Cannon failed to fire. First round entered breech and jammed preventing breech from clearing.

(*In Chris Shores *'Those Other Eagles'* he records the Ju88 as an aircraft of 3(F)/122).

Above: Tommy Cody hoisted high by his squadron colleagues following the combat of 28 January 1943.

IMPERIAL WAR MUSEUM SOUND ARCHIVE (www.iwm.org.uk)

Left: 'Pilot Officer Tommy Cody returns following a successful combat. A selection of stills from footage taken at the time shows the elation.

Tommy Cody would follow up his first success with two further claims against enemy aircraft. The first took place on 13 February 1943.

FROM: RAF Station Coltishall
TO: Headquarter Fighter Command RAF Bentley Priory, Stanmore Middx
               Headquarters No. 12 Group, RAF Watnall, Notts.
DATE: 13 February 1943
               167 Gold Coast Squadron and 118 Squadron
               167 Sqn - 9 L.R. Spits VB, 3 Spits VC
               118 Sqn - 12 L.R. Spits VB
TIME: 1600 - 1605 hrs
               Ijmuiden
CONDITIONS: 4/10 cloud at 3,000 feet. Visibility 20 miles.

General report
167 Squadron were A/B from Ludham at 1520 hrs and rendezvoused with 12 Venturas ref No. 2 Group and 118 Squadron from Coltishall. 118 Sqdn were A/B from Coltishall at 1510 hrs, rendezvous being effected at Mundesly at 200 feet by the three formations. 118 Sqdn were acting as escort cover and 167 as escort.

Course was set at 1527 hours on 110 M at zero feet at 190/200 IAS. After 22 minutes course was altered to 102 magnetic and the formation climbed at 165 IAS for 10 minutes, landfall being made by bombers and escort 10 miles south of Ijmuiden at 1547 hrs, at this time 118 Sqdn was flying in formation of six sections of 2 a/c, each section in line astern and spread well out. L.R. tanks were jettisoned 10 miles before reaching the Dutch coast which was crossed at 10,000 feet.

As the bombers and escort swept inland, 118 Squadron positioned themselves, in the sun at 12,000 feet, patrolling South to North along the coast, approaching Ijmuiden out of the sun.

Just before bombers approached the target 8 FW190s made a head on attack on the bombers at extreme range of 1,000 yds, the close escort diving through them, the bombers being subjected to fairly accurate and moderately intense and light flak. Bombs were released at approximately 1600 hours and were seen to fall in the dock area straddling three ships moored along the southern quay. The rearmost ship, a merchant vessel of about 8,000 tons received a direct hit amidships and other bombs fell in the water scoring near misses.

On completion of the bombing run the formation dived sharply to sea level and 4 FW190s were seen positioning themselves to port and above the bombers for a further attack. 118 Sqdn formed 3 sections of 4 a/c, red section followed by yellow section, diving down on these a/c, while Blue section remained above as cover. Three of the FWs then dived for the coast at fast speed the fourth diving across the top of the bomber formation from SW to NE, firing a short burst which passed above them and then, climbing steeply followed by Red Section.

Red 1 F/Lt Newberry DFC got in a 2 - second burst of cannon and M.G. from 600 to 500 yards rear starboard quarter, using camera gun but without observing any result. He was then followed by Red 3, Sgt Smith, who gave a 2 second burst of cannon and m/g from 600 yards from port rear quarter, and Red 4, P/O Watson, put in a 3 second burst of cannon and m/g from 400 yards, on rear port quarter, both using camera guns but failing to see results.

All these attacks were made between 500 and 3,000 feet and although Spits climbed on full boost when attacking, were unable to compare with the rate of climb of the FW. It initially got into cloud cover and was last seen with black smoke pouring from its exhaust, but no claims made.

During the head on attack on the bombers P/O Cody of 167 Sqn gave a 3 second burst from quarter starboard astern with cannon and m.g. from 300 yards at FW which turned on its back and dived to port without results being seen. It was at this time that P/O Cody felt strikes in the tail of his aircraft, which is now reported to have been from cannon and m.g. and not from flak as previously thought by Engineer Officer.

F/Lt Hall and P/O Gordon climbed to attack two FWs which however dived away. In the second attack, by four FWs F/Lt Hall got in a 2 second burst with m.g. at one E/A at extreme range, no results being seen.

All three squadrons returned in formation at sea level, both Spitfire Squadrons, landing at their respective bases at 1700 hours.

Observations

One red flak pointer was put up from a point 3 miles south of Ijmuiden just before the bombing run was made. The FW190s were firing a self-explosive type of shell, and they used tip and run tactics, being exceptionally fast in the climb.

i Further details on Tommy Cody's flying career can be found in Chris Shores's outstanding piece of work *Those Other Eagles* (*A tribute to the British, Common - wealth and Free European Fighter Pilots who claimed between two and four victories in aerial combat, 1939 – 1982*).

'Tommy' Cody was credited with a FW190 damaged, and a few months later he would add to his confirmed tally. On 3 May 1943, again with No. 118 Squadron, the 12 Spitfires of No. 167 Squadron (a mixture of VBs and VCs – Tommy Cody flying a VB) were providing escort to 12 Venturas bombing a power station at Amsterdam. After taking off at 1650 hours, rendezvous was made over Coltishall and the bombers began to climb, but just prior to reaching bombing height a swarm of enemy aircraft arrived and, as the returning pilots would inform their intelligence officer, 'Many dog-fights ensued.' Tommy Cody was right in the thick of it, as recorded in his combat report and backed up by that of a fellow pilot.

PERSONAL COMBAT REPORT OF F/O CTK CODY ON 3 MAY 1943

I was Yellow 1. At the peak of the climb, 11,000 feet, and approximately 6 miles from Ijmuiden, the Squadron was attacked by 20+ FW190s. The Squadron broke port through 360 degrees. Immediately afterwards the Squadron was broken again falling behind and to port of the bombers. This break separated my Section from the Squadron and we were approximately 10 miles inland on the outskirts of Amsterdam.

I with my Section, tried to rejoin, but had lost too much ground. I knew that the bombers would be coming out over Ijmuiden, so I took my Section there. I was at once attacked by 8 FW190s in sections of two's. I broke first left then right according to the direction of each attack. Then 2 came in from the port and one to the starboard. I broke left, and Yellow 3 broke right, as he was being fired at. After this break, two came in at 7 o'clock above. I pulled my nose up and gave 1 ring deflection for 1 second without observing results. The range was about 400-500 yards. I changed to line astern and fired at the same range for 2 seconds observing black smoke streaming from the e/a. He slowly stalled to port and dived down. I observed no more at the time owing to repeated attacks. A few moments later I saw an a/c burning in the sea just below, approximately 3 miles out to sea South of Ijmuiden. This is substantiated by Yellow 3, P/O Van Hamel (Dutch), who saw the black smoke from the e/a and then saw an a/c burning in the sea in the approximate position. At first I thought this was Yellow 3, who had lost me just after the combat, but as I later heard him call up, I believe that it was my FW190.

Yellow 2 and myself returned to base followed at sea level for 40 miles by 4 FW190s.

Owing to the evidence of other pilots, I claim this FW190 as destroyed*. Camera-gun carried and exposed.

PERSONAL COMBAT REPORT OF P/O VAN HAMEL (DUTCH) ON 3 MAY 1943

I was flying Yellow 3. Referring to the above report of F/O Cody, at the point where Yellow 1 and 2 broke left, I broke to the right, as 1 FW190 was diving on me from 500 yards from 4 o'clock. I became separated from yellow 1 and 2, and I saw one FW190 coming down with black smoke coming from it. After a few turns, I was alone and was attacked by 3 FW190s; 2 of them attacked first and after turning into them the other FW190 made a head on attack at me and fired. I fired back but did not give enough deflection, and one e/a passed me at 100 yards, and I got in a short burst of cannon and machine gun, but had to break off as the other 2 e/a attacked me again from 6 o'clock. This lasted about 10 minutes, and I decided to return to base.

Tommy Cody would have his claim of one FW190 destroyed confirmed. ∎

(*In Chris Shores's *Those Other Eagles* he records the FW190 as an aircraft of II/JG 1.)

Chivalry over Sicily

High above Sicily a Luftwaffe Focke-Wulf 190 pilot finds a Royal Air Force Spitfire, flown by 232 Squadron's Eddie McCann, defenceless, and at his mercy.

Eddie McCann was in trouble. Serious trouble. The Focke-Wulf 190 had swung in behind and there was nothing Eddie could do. The wing of his Spitfire was already badly damaged and Eddie daren't try any evasive manoeuvres. When the Luftwaffe pilot unleashed his cannon, Eddie's view of his enemy changed forever.

Eddie McCann joined No. 232 Squadron in the cauldron of North Africa in April 1943, flying operationally during the squeeze of the Axis forces from East and West, and their ultimate defeat in Tunisia. Eddie had flown in hostile skies in the UK prior to his move to the desert, but he had seen little action. Over the Mediterranean he would!

Operation Husky

With North Africa in the hands of the Allies in May 1943, offensive intentions moved towards the invasion of Sicily. No. 232 Squadron moved to Ta Kali, Malta, at the end of the month, and in the run-up to the launch of Operation Husky, the re-entry into Europe through Sicily, Eddie's main task would be escorting Spitfires, Mitchells, and Marauders, the main opposition coming from flak.

When the invasion began on 10 July Eddie flew with his colleagues numerous times over the Mediterranean island and would record 'SFA' against the sorties in his logbook, along with, 'The Axis seem to have their fingers well in.'

But on 16 July the fingers came out, and Eddie would be entering in his logbook, 'Wizard show, bounced by 15+ Me109s'.

Eddie, flying as Blue 2 on a patrol of Catania took off at 1830 hours that evening. Three-quarters of an hour later, '15 plus Me109s bounced the squadron from out of the sun. In the ensuing melee, Blue 1 and myself chased two 109s for some distance but had to give up the chase as we were being outdistanced. Blue 1, however, managed to get strikes on the rear one.' Eddie headed back to join the rest of his squadron and on the way, 'we saw three more 109s which we chased. Again we were outdistanced'. Again his colleague managed to register strikes on one. Again they tried to rejoin their squadron colleagues, 'when we saw two more 109s coming head on at us from out of the sun. Blue 1 decided to attack the one nearest to him and I the other one. As the closing speed of the aircraft was very high, I decided to turn and get on the tail of the 109 before opening fire. I had the chance of making a deflection shot but did not fire as Blue 1 was in the line of fire so I waited till I got dead astern of the 109 by which time the enemy aircraft was 300 yards away and gave it a three second burst. I observed strikes on the wing roots. I continued to follow the enemy aircraft down but he increased his angle of dive and easily outdistanced

EDDIE McCANN

Right: Eddie McCann's logbook records the attack on his airfield, and his encounter with the Luftwaffe the following day. **Centre:** Eddie's Spitfire V, April 1943 **Far Right:** Eddie McCann, early 1945, whilst serving at an operational training unit.

STEVE DARLOW

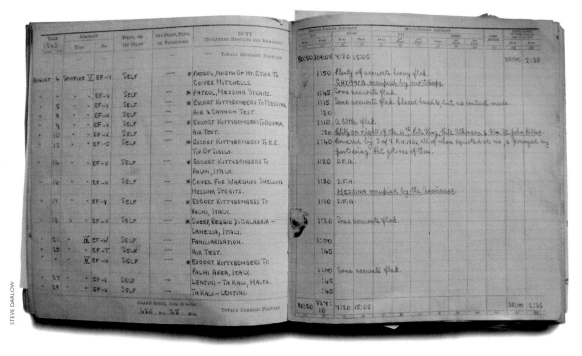

me. The last I saw of the 109 was in a 70 degree dive at 7,000 feet when he was lost in the haze. I then broke away.' Eddie was later credited with one Me109 damaged.

Fighting at the front line
As the Allied ground forces advanced through Sicily, air force squadrons deployed to the island in the Army's wake, No. 232 Squadron arriving at Lentini on 22 July. Eddie recorded in his logbook, 'Just over 10 miles to the front line'. Operational duties continued to the end of the month and into August, escorts and patrols, the opposition, in the main, coming from ground fire. The young flyers of No. 232 Squadron were becoming frustrated. On 10 August the No. 232 Squadron ORB recorded: 'From the continual complaining of the pilots in the squadron that they very rarely contact enemy aircraft while on their escort duties, sweeps and patrols, it is becoming evident that something is seriously wrong with the morale and efficiency of the German Air Force and it is gratifying to record that no pilots or aircraft have been lost during the month through enemy action in the air.'

But on 11 August the Luftwaffe would prove to Eddie and his colleagues that they were not yet defeated. Eddie recalls: 'The day before, I wasn't on the actual mission, but I had gone down to the landing strip. We were just sitting around and we heard an aeroplane. I thought somebody

with engine trouble had come back. I looked up and there was a Me109. I thought, "Hells Bells, what's he doing here?" He was obviously reconnoitring the area.'

At 2230 hours on 11 August the Luftwaffe followed up the reconnaissance of the previous day and paid Lentini another visit. Some slight warning was given as flares were dropped over the airfield, then explosives and incendiaries fell. The No. 232 Squadron diary recorded: 'Unfortunately personnel on the domestic site, instead of remaining and taking such cover as the sites provided (i.e. trees, vehicles, and an inadequate number of slit trenches), streamed out in order to take cover in an orange grove, situated at the foot of a hill on the south side of the camp. To do this they had to cross open ground and it is thought that they were observed by enemy bomber crews as the place was brilliantly lit up by the flares. In consequence a stick of bombs was put across this stretch of ground.'

Eddie recalls: 'Our domestic site was a little way away from the airfield. We were living in a little wood. When we realised what was happening, the ack-ack was firing. We thought well we better get under cover just in case. Things started to get very uncomfortable. One or two of the chaps decided to make a run for it to get more protection. They started running from the domestic site down to a ditch at the bottom of the hill. Just at that time a German night

SOUK-EL-KHEMIS.
(APRIL 1943)

EDDIE McCANN

fighter came over and dropped a bomb, which struck and killed several of the chaps as they were running down.'

Seven men lost their lives – LAC D Evans, LAC O Rigney, LAC E Russell, LAC L Jarvis, Pilot Officer Vernon St John, Flight Sergeant Pete King, and Flight Sergeant Wilfred Atkinson.

Avenging lost friends
The following day, the squadron diary recorded: 'the burial of those killed in the air raid was carried out on a site situated to the north-west of the camp. The Service was carried out by the Wing C. of E. Padre and it is understood that the site will be converted into a proper cemetery.'

The pilots of No. 232 Squadron now had to come to terms with directly witnessing the loss of their friends. If there was a feeling of revenge, then the following day would provide an opportunity and Eddie would come face to face with his enemy. Eddie was one of four No. 232 Squadron pilots involved in the escort of 'Kittybombers to the north east tip of Sicily, at that time the flak concentration was so hard that we steered well clear of it'.

Eddie recalls: 'We were flying up and down just north of Sicily across the Mediterranean, and we were suddenly bounced by 7 Focke-Wulf 190s. The funny thing is that I reported these aircraft flying east to west ahead of us, about 12 o'clock high, and the aircraft nearest us said it's all right they're friendly. I feel convinced that these were the Focke-Wulf's that eventually bounced us, as they were going into the sun and came down a few minutes later. Somebody called to me to break quickly – I was on the outside. I tried to break as quickly as I could, to starboard, but the cannons from this Focke-Wulf smashed into the port wing. I think the call probably saved my life. A split second sooner and I'm sure it would have hit the cockpit. It all happened so quickly I didn't have time to think.'

Eddie was now flying a damaged aircraft and he couldn't be sure to what extent; he made the decision to try and get back to his airfield. 'I didn't dare risk going because of the flak concentration. I decided to go round the other side of Mount Etna back to Lentini. I was taking great care. Then whilst flying back across the Mediterranean towards the coast a Focke-Wulf came up behind me. I thought, "Oh Christ"; I daren't manoeuvre in case anything went wrong.'

The Luftwaffe pilot closed in on Eddie, but instead of blasting him from the sky he took up a position in formation with his RAF adversary. 'Then he fired off his cannons to show me that he could still shoot. Clearly he could see that I was badly damaged and he must have felt it was not the thing to do, to knock me out. After a few seconds he flew off and I was left to fly back to base. That one event made me change my opinion of the Luftwaffe.' ■

Right: On 30 April 1943, No. 600 Squadron's Flight Sergeant Alwyn Downing (left) and his navigator/radar operator Sergeant John Lyons (right) would carry out one of the most successful Beaufighter attacks of the entire war. Downing would become an 'Ace in a Day'.

No. 600 'CITY OF LONDON' Squadron, Auxilliary Air Force began the war operating with Blenheim Ifs in daylight. On 10 May 1940 the squadron lost of 5 out of 6 aircraft on a raid to Waalhaven airfield, Holland. Conversion to a night fighter role soon followed and the squadron received Beaufighter Ifs in September 1940. In November 1942 the squadron moved to North Africa, operating in the night defence of ports and airfields whilst the Allies swept the Axis troops into Tunisia. To date the squadron had only 17 victories to its name, but in the next seven months that score would triple, with further success during the Italian campaign. One RAF team at the centre of such success was Alwyn Downing and John Lyons.

'This brilliant feat...'

The combat report opposite describes a particularly devastating attack. Although this was a somewhat exceptional sortie, Downing and Lyons both receiving the Distinguished Flying Medal, Downing's squadron colleagues had also been very successful in the preceding weeks. As the squadron reporter recorded: 'This brilliant feat brought the squadron's score in the present campaign to 32, of which 18 had been obtained during the month of April.' Further success came the squadron's way in May, and Downing and Lyons would claim a Ju52/3m on the night of 8/9 May.

History now shows that Hitler and Mussolini's decision to reinforce the failing defensive struggle in Tunisia, by air, was a major tactical error. Not only did their obstinacy hand over hundreds of thousands of Axis troops to the Allies, diminishing their ability to defend Sicily and Italy, it also decimated Luftwaffe transport units, with the resultant loss of trained aircrews.

Ace in a Day

In April 1943 the Axis forces in Tunisia were under siege, with their backs to the Mediterranean. Reinforcements were despatched, by air, in a futile attempt to prevent the inevitable. But the cost in employing such a measure was excessively high.

COMBAT REPORT
30 April
Beaufighter Mk VI [V8755 'Q'], AI Mk VII
Pilot - Flight Sergeant A. B. Downing
N/Rad - Sergeant J. Lyons
Took off from Bone 0330 hours. Landed Bone 0615 hours.

At 0330 hours F/Sgt A.B. Downing with Sgt J. Lyons Nav/Rad, then operating with No. 153 Squadron on Beaufighters, was given vectors by Cap Serrat C.O.L. onto bandits travelling north 30 miles south of Sardinia.

Patrolled for Forfar. Orbited a flashing light on the sea some 30 - 40 miles north of Cap Takouch obtaining a momentary contact dead below. Decreased height to 3,000 feet but no further contact obtained and Beau then given vectors 110 degrees then 130 degrees. Taken over by Skemer. Told bandits very low and slow 100 miles east travelling north-east. Beau told to go full out and decrease height to 500 feet on vector 060 degrees and then 040 degrees. To keep within range of Skemer Beau climbed to 3,500 feet, then to 8,500 feet. At latter height told bandit 2 miles ahead very low but Beau getting out of C O L range and no further help possible.

AI then failed but Beau dived down to sea-level and continued on 040 degrees all out. Red of dawn now appearing and pilot saw a small dot ahead and slightly to starboard. Beau skimming waves closed in behind and slightly below. Identified a/c as Ju52 and from 200 yards dead astern fired a short burst hitting Ju52 on fuselage and wing roots. Enemy aircraft instantly blew up and went into the sea leaving a large patch of flame on the water. Beau orbited the fire and N/R observed 3 more dots to the south.

Beau closed and 3 Ju52's were seen in rough echelon starboard formation some half mile apart flying NNE very low. Beau got in behind nearest enemy aircraft. From 600 yards enemy aircraft opened fire from top of fuselage. No hits felt on Beau which closed in and from 200 - 300 yards dead astern fired a short burst hitting starboard engine. Beau then swung away and closing in fired another short burst hitting port engine and petrol tanks. Enemy aircraft went up in flames and skidded into the sea burning fiercely.

Beau then closed in on next enemy aircraft which weaved violently and opened fire again from great range. Beau fired from 400 yards astern but just clipped enemy aircraft and strikes were seen on the sea low and ahead. Beau closed, enemy aircraft still firing, to 150 yards and fired a short burst. Starboard wing of enemy aircraft holed and glow observed internally. Flashes were seen also on top gun position and fire ceased from that quarter. Beau now alongside. Enemy aircraft burning but fire experience from side guns, 2 bullets going through Beau's tail. Beau turned but enemy aircraft now seen burning fiercely on the water.

Beau now closed in behind fourth enemy aircraft, which also weaved, and opened fire with one short burst from 200 yards astern securing hits on the wing roots. Beau passed over above as enemy aircraft ditched burning in the water. Pilot orbiting saw dinghy and 20 or more men with yellow skullcaps in the water.

At the same time another Ju52 was seen. Again at 600 yards as Beau was closing in behind, enemy aircraft opened fire from top gun. Beau closed to 200 yards dead astern and fired a short burst. Enemy aircraft instantly blew up and fell into the sea in flames. Beau orbited seeing the 5 patches of flame on the sea and the dinghy from the fourth. Beau orbited for some time. Light was now good but nothing further seen.

The 5 Ju52's were destroyed between 0455 hours and 0505 hours the first 4 in 6 minutes and combat took place some 30 miles south of Cagliari. Speed of Ju52s was 160 mph and height 0 - 100 feet. Beau now at sea-level returned on 190 degrees then 240 degrees and 235 degrees passing south of La Galite. Weather overcast by 8 - 9/10 medium and high cloud. Visibility good with slight sea haze. Rounds fired - 490 cannon, 990 m/g. 150 rounds for each of 3 cannon and 40 rounds for 4th cannon blast tube of which hit by enemy fire. Damage to Beaufighter superficial but damage to blast tube with shrapnel effect suggests gun of heavier calibre than m/g. Camouflage of Ju52s mottled grey. No dustbin below. Claim 5 Ju52s destroyed.

Operation Shingle

As 1943 closed out, Sicily had been taken, Italy had capitulated, and the Allies had landed on the Italian mainland, and were fighting their way up the peninsula. But the invading armies were meeting stiff German opposition. Into the New Year and the Allies launched an attempt to outflank the stagnated front line with an amphibious landing in the German rear, at Anzio, south of Rome – Operation Shingle. On 22 January British and American troops, virtually unopposed, filed off the landing craft onto the Anzio beaches. In the following days whilst the beachhead was secured, the Germans redeployed troops to oppose the landing. Hemmed in at Anzio the supply shipping became a prime target for the Luftwaffe and No. 600 Squadron was tasked to counter this threat. On 26 January 1944, Alwyn Downing and John Lyons would make a most significant contribution, as the combat report shown right testifies, claiming two He177s and one Ju88.

Right: Alwyn Downing would not have the monopoly on success at No. 600 Squadron during the campaigns in Tunisia, Sicily, and Italy. His squadron colleagues also got to grips with the enemy. One distinguished 'claimant' was the squadron commanding officer Wing Commander C P 'Paddy' Green, notably shooting down four Ju88s on the night of 14/15 July 1943. Here Paddy looks out of the cockpit of Bristol Beaufighter Mark VIF, V8762 'A' (equipped with AI Mark IV).

Another extraordinary sortie. Downing and Lyons both received the award of the Distinguished Flying Cross in March, but in the meantime tragedy had struck. On the night of 31 January/1 February 1944 Alwyn and John were forced to bale out of their Beaufighter following engine failure, coming down into the sea. Alwyn was rescued but John Lyons was lost. Alwyn Downing returned to the UK and in February 1945 began flying Mosquitoes with No. 169 Squadron, surviving the war. ∎

● 31-year-old Pilot Officer John Thomas Lyons DFC, DFM is buried at Naples War Cemetery – Grave/ Memorial Reference: I. G. 2.

ℹ Further information on Alwyn Downing can be found in Chris Shores and Clive Williams *Aces High* and Chris Shores's *Aces High Volume 2*.

Time	Height	Area
17:25 – 17:30	6,000 feet	N of Capri
17:45	6,000 feet	8 mile NW of Circeo Pt.
17:50	4,000 feet	10 mile NW of Circeo Pt.
17:54	6,000 feet	NW of Circeo
17:56	8,000 feet	15 mile NW of Circeo Pt.
19:05	12,000 feet	Rome area
19:07	12,500 feet	Anzio area
19:08	12,500 feet	Anzio area
19:16	10,000 feet	Anzio area
19:20	10,000 feet	28 miles NW of Anzio
19:30	10,000 feet	Anzio harbour

COMBAT REPORT. 26 January 1944, Gaudo airfield, Beaufighter Mk. VIF AI Mk. IV, Up 1710, Down 2010, Captain Flying Officer A. B. Downing DFM, Crew Pilot Officer J. T. Lyons DFM, Defensive patrol, Cloud - nil, Visibility - good, General weather - starlight, dark.

Called sector 'Changer'
Heard sector 'Grubsteak' informing 'Gugnunk' aircraft of trade in Anzio area.
Bustered [full speed] north calling G.C.I. [Ground Controlled Interception] 'Project'

Told bandit very close. Head-on contact obtained at same time and visual simultaneously on aircraft identified as He177 passing beneath. Beaufighter took diving turn to regain visual and enemy aircraft opened fire but obtained no strikes. Beaufighter turning in on enemy aircraft's tail, stalled and nearly spun. Came out and made beam attack ending up dead astern firing 4 snap bursts (with little or no deflection). Strikes were seen on fuselage, port engine and under-gun position. Last burst fired into port wing roots.

Enemy aircraft caught fire and crashed into sea. Confirmed by G.C.I. 'Project'. Beaufighter continued on northerly course. G.C.I. 'Project' unable to help.

Freelance contact obtained at maximum range on aircraft starboard and above but target went out of range. 'Window' was being dropped, but Beaufighter followed through and again obtained contact at maximum range on bandit flying north west. Visual on aircraft at 5,000 feet range flying at 4,000 feet. Closed in identifying He177. From 200 yards dead astern fired long burst.

Enemy aircraft returned fire from upper and lower guns without result, but enemy aircraft immediately burst into flames and crashed with blinding flash near the beach where it was seen to continue burning. Confirmed by G.C.I. 'Project'.

Beaufighter then flew north under 'Project' control raid having petered out. No damage to shipping had been observed. 2 searchlights crossing were observed between Rome and the Tiber mouth.

Vectored after stray raid in Rome area. Fleeting contact obtained. Recalled by 'Project' to intercept main raids flying south. Flew towards Anzio experiencing 'window'. 'Project' now unable to help further.

Experienced flak from ship which ceased fire immediately when colours fired. Orbited flares over 'Shingle' area and out to sea.

Given northerly vector by 'Project' towards bandit said to be 6 miles ahead at 12,000 feet. Contact obtained at maximum range but weak - Beaufighter therefore remained under control until good blip was obtained at 9,000 feet range dead ahead and 20 - 25 degrees below.

Closed to minimum range on target doing 200 - 240 IAS and obtained visual, though with difficulty owing to oxygen failure. Closed further seeing 4 exhausts and Ju88 silhouette. Got on to tail of enemy aircraft and with visual blurred fired short burst from 100 yards dead astern and slightly below. Strikes observed. Enemy aircraft weaved and lost speed and smoke was seen pouring from starboard engine. Pilot had difficulty in holding visual owing to low speed (110 IAS) of enemy aircraft and weaving. Fired medium skidding burst from astern and slightly below at less than 100 yards range.

Port petrol tank of aircraft exploded and Ju88 crashed in flames into the sea where it was seen to burn for a long period. No 'window' was experienced during the interception.

Saw ship on fire and explosions.
Total claim - 2 He177s destroyed, 1 Ju88 destroyed

We Still Remember

"Mary Ruth" Memories of Mobile crew. Kneeling from the left: James P. Feerick, bombardier; William R. Brown, tail gunner. Standing, from the left: Henry 'Maurice' Crain, ball turret gunner; Raymond Litzo, right waist gunner; James O. Akers, flight engineer/ top turret gunner; William 'Glenn' Allen, left waist gunner; Richard O. Maculley, radio operator; Vincent J. Bliley, navigator; Kenneth L. Brown, pilot; James H. Quenin, co-pilot. Sgts Allen and Maculley were killed when the "Mary Ruth" was shot down on 22 June 1943.

Below right:
Loren and Mary Ruth Roll, wedding photo; March 1943. While flying No. 42-29536 to England in March 1943, First Lieutenant Loren Roll and his crew had to stay over in Mobile, AL, for several days whilst the aircraft underwent repairs. On Friday 12 March, he met Mary Ruth King in his hotel lounge. They began talking and then dated for the next week. On Friday the 19th they were married. The crew arranged to have painted on the nose of the plane, *"Mary Ruth" Memories of Mobile*. Loren and his crew flew No. 536 on to England, via Brazil and North Africa, leaving her at an English air base in southern England. They never saw No. 536 again for another crew would fly her into battle.

Unsurprisingly many bomber crews developed a special bond with their weapons of war. After all, they had to trust their steed to carry them safely to, in, and from combat. American crews often showed their affection by personalising the bombers with a name and nose art, many chosen to represent happier memories of home. One such was *"Mary Ruth" Memories of Mobile* and here, guest contributor **Lowell L. Getz**, provides us with the story behind the name and the fate of the aircraft and the men who flew her.

There was an unusual sense of anticipation at one of the hardstands at USAAF Station 121, otherwise known as Bassingbourn, England, that early Monday morning of 17 May 1943. On the hardstand was B-17F Flying Fortress, No. 41-24485, *Memphis Belle*, 324th Bombardment Squadron, 91st Bombardment Group (Heavy), VIII Bomber Command.

Crew Chief Master Sergeant Joseph M. Giambrone was busily overseeing the last-minute ground crew maintenance work. Today's mission, to the German U-boat pens at Lorient, France, was special for the crew of the *Memphis Belle*. If they returned, the pilot, Captain Robert K. Morgan, and his ten-man crew would have completed 25 combat missions. Anyone completing 25 missions would not fly any more combat and be sent back to the States by VIII Bomber Command. *Memphis Belle* would fly her own 25th mission two days later when First Lieutenant Clayton L. Anderson and his crew flew her to the U-boat yards at Kiel, Germany.

Major William Wyler (the renowned Hollywood movie director) and Hollywood cameraman, Captain William Clothier, had flown several missions on the *Memphis Belle*, including one to Heligoland Island the previous Saturday, to film air combat action. On 13 June Captain Morgan and his crew would leave Bassingbourn to fly the *Memphis Belle* back to the States. There they would receive three months of well-earned public acclaim at War Bond rallies throughout the country. From film taken on Saturday and on the other missions, Major Wyler would produce the highly acclaimed documentary movie, *The Memphis Belle*.

At nearby Bassingbourn hardstand that same Monday morning, another ground crew, headed by Master Sergeant Bert 'Black Jack' Pierce, 28, from Harrison, Arkansas, was also busily engaged. They were preparing B-17F Flying Fortress No. 42-29536, *"Mary Ruth"* *Memories of Mobile*, 401st Squadron of the 91st Group, for today's mission to Lorient.

Just regular guys
The crew quietly went about its pre-flight routines. The flight deck crew: pilot, First Lieutenant Kenneth L. Brown, 24, Hodgenville, Kentucky, previously an Aircraft Armorer Staff Sergeant; co-pilot, Second Lieutenant James H. Quenin, 26, Fort Smith, Arkansas, formerly a Signal Corps Sergeant. The nose crew: navigator, Second Lieutenant Vincent J. Bliley, 26, Ottumwa, Iowa, a former staff artist

for the Ottumwa, *Iowa Courier*, bombardier, Second Lieutenant James P. Feerick, 24, New York City, who earlier had completed a year's enlistment in the 102nd Engineers, 47th Division, New York National Guard. The rest of the crew: flight engineer and top turret gunner, Technical Sergeant James O. Akers, 23, Starbuck, Minnesota, a construction worker in Idaho when he enlisted; radioman, Technical Sergeant Richard O. Maculley, 19, Chester, Pennsylvania, recognised for his artistic abilities, who left High School at the age of 17 to enlist; ball turret gunner, Staff Sergeant Henry 'Maurice' Crain, 41, 'Pops' of the group, originally from Canyon, Texas, with a Bachelor's Degree in Journalism from the University of Texas, who had been working as a city editor for the *New York Daily News* and as a literary agent; left waist gunner, Staff Sergeant William 'Glenn' Allen, 21, Athens, Georgia, who was operating two small neighborhood grocery stores when he entered the Service; right waist gunner, Staff Sergeant Raymond Litzo, 22, Denver, Colorado, who was attending the University of Denver, majoring in Business Administration and a member of the golf team when he left school to join the Army Air Corps; tail gunner, Staff Sergeant William R. Brown, 22, Eldorado, Illinois, who had been working for a PepsiCola distributorship.

Combat missions

There was nothing unique about *"Mary Ruth" Memories of Mobile* to attract the attention of a Hollywood director. Today's mission would be only her third over enemy territory. The nose painting was not sufficiently artistic to warrant inclusion in any of the books that would appear in later years depicting 'nose artwork' of military aircraft. There was no painting of a perky bathing beauty such as *Memphis Belle*. Rather, there was simply *"Mary Ruth" Memories of Mobile* in plain block dark yellow letters. No. 536 had been named by an unknown crew back in the States. When Lieutenant Brown and his crew were assigned the already-named plane, superstition prevented them from making a change.

"Mary Ruth" Memories of Mobile would fly four more combat missions. On 29 May she would fly to 'flak city', St Nazaire, France.

On 11 June the *"Mary Ruth"* would attempt to go to the docks of Bremen, Germany. When Bremen was found to be clouded over, the Group would divert to Wilhelmshaven. The day *Memphis Belle* and her crew would leave Bassingbourn to return home to the States,

LOREN ROLL

Left: Original nose art of *"Mary Ruth" Memories of Mobile*. Loren Roll had the nose art placed on his plane at the repair facility in Mobile after he and Mary Ruth King were married.

RAY BOWDEN

Below left: Another close-up of the nose art of *"Mary Ruth" Memories of Mobile*. The original nose art letters were over-painted in block yellow, but retaining the original letter sizes, by the paint and fabric shop at Bassingbourn when she arrived there, and was assigned to the 401st Squadron.

JOE HARLICK

Left: St Nazaire, 29 May 1943: strike photos, as the bombs were hitting. The *"Mary Ruth"* flew the No. 2 position (right wing of the lead plane) in the No. 2 element of the high squadron on this mission. Note the precision of the bombs in hitting the sub pens; a few are exploding in the water immediately in front of the openings to the pens.

Right: B-17F No. 536, *"Mary Ruth" Memories of Mobile,* on a combat mission to Huls, Germany, 22 June 1943. She was shot down later on this mission. The B-17 in the upper left, No. 475, *"Stric-Nine",* was shot down over the Channel 10 July 1943. The plane from which the picture was taken, No. 069, *"Our Gang",* was shot down 17 August 1943.

"Mary Ruth" Memories of Mobile once again would fly to Bremen. This time she would be successful. On 22 June *Memphis Belle* and her crew would wind up their three-day 'tour kick-off' celebration in Memphis, Tennessee. Earlier that day the now sleek *"Mary Ruth"* would become a scattered pile of smoking rubble in a forest 4 kilometers west of the small village of Wulfen in the Ruhr Valley of Germany. *"Mary Ruth" Memories of Mobile* would not quite make it to her final target, the synthetic chemical plant at Huls.

Frontal attack

Three flights of two FW190s in a frontal attack from slightly high off the right wing of *"Mary Ruth",* about ten degrees to the right, would set the No. 4 engine afire, damage the cockpit flight controls, and knock out much of the electrical system. *"Mary Ruth"* would drop out of formation. From all sides, FW190s would then attack the now alone *"Mary Ruth",* their 20mm cannon shells exploding in the cockpit destroying more controls. The bail-out bell would be rung. Sergeant Akers would leave the top turret just before it blew up, throwing exploding ammunition into the cockpit. Lieutenant Brown would struggle to hold the plane level as the right wing burned away, all the while exploding shells, sent fragments of

the instrument panels into his head and face. Lieutenant Feerick would make two frenzied trips from the bombardier compartment to the bomb bay to work on the shackle mechanisms of two bombs with a screwdriver, eventually causing them to fall free. This would allow the forward crew to escape by squeezing around the unsalvoed bombs. Lieutenant Brown's efforts would buy time for the rear crew to get to their escape hatches. For his efforts on behalf of the crew, Lieutenant Brown would be awarded the Distinguished Flying Cross. Before all the crew could bail out, the outer wing would blow-off throwing *"Mary Ruth"* into a spinning downward dive, the centrifugal force of which would prevent the remaining crew from leaving the plane. Almost immediately thereafter the *"Mary Ruth"* would explode, throwing free all but Sergeants Allen and Maculley, who would remain trapped within the falling fuselage.

End of the line

In a few minutes it would all be over. *"Mary Ruth" Memories of Mobile* would be no more. Sergeants Maculley and Allen would lie dead in the wreckage. The remainder of the crew would float to the earth and soon be prisoners of war. Lieutenant Brown and Sergeant Crain would manage to evade capture for five days before being taken prisoner. Lieutenant Quenin would sustain compound fractures of both legs when his parachute opened. His legs would escape further injury when landing as he would fall through the tile roof of a farm shed on his shoulder and be suspended above the floor by the parachute. But, he would be shot through one of his legs whilst being captured by German infantry.

The officers would be sent to the South Compound of Stalag Luft III near Sagan, Silesia, spending most of their time in captivity. Because of the severity of his injuries, Lieutenant Quenin would be removed from Stalag Luft III on 16 February 1944 and repatriated through Lisbon, Portugal, arriving back in the United States on 15 March 1944. On 27 January 1945, Lieutenants Bliley, Brown, and Feerick would be forced by the Germans to take part in a freezing cold 'Death March' and then packed in small train cars en route to Stalag VII-A at Moosburg near Munich. There they would be liberated by Patton's Third Army on 29 April. The enlisted crew would first be sent to Stalag VII-A at Moosburg. After six months they would be moved in railroad box cars to Stalag XVII-B near Krems, Austria, and held there until early April 1945. They then would be marched up the Danube river to Braunau, Austria, where they would be liberated by advancing Americans.

Homecoming

There would be no War Bond rallies or heroes welcome for the crew of *"Mary Ruth" Memories of Mobile* when they returned. Only families and friends celebrated their homecoming. Lieutenant Brown remained in the Air Force to fly B-29s in Korea and B-52s in Vietnam, eventually retiring as a Colonel. He obtained a Master's Degree from the University of Arizona. Afterwards he served as an administrator in the University Medical School until retiring again, this time to his golf game in La Jolla, California. Lieutenant Quenin recovered from his injuries to return to flight status to fly in the Berlin Airlift. Later he served as Director of Materiel for the 505 Tactical Air Control Group, and flew a few 'unofficial' missions, in Vietnam, finally retiring, as a Lieutenant Colonel, to sell real-estate in Costa Mesa, California. Lieutenant Bliley returned to civilian life to own and operate an oil distributorship in Milwaukie, Oregon. Lieutenant Feerick became a Captain in the New York Fire Department and later served as an administrator at Mt Sinai Hospital, and then as an Ordained Deacon in the Catholic Church.

Sergeant Akers remained in the Army when the Air Force split away, serving in Korea, retiring as a Warrant Officer to Colorado Springs, Colorado, where he would engage in a number of business ventures and work for the US Postal Service. Sergeant Brown remained in the Air Force as a supply sergeant, eventually retiring to become manager of the P. N. Hirsch Department Store in Humbolt, Tennessee. Sergeant Crain returned to New York to resume his pre-war activities as a literary agent, operating his own agency. Sergeant Litzo returned to Denver to work for Boyd Distributing, a major appliance distributorship, and to continue his avocation with golf. Sergeant Pierce left

AGNES DAVIS

RON RAAIJMAKERS

Left: The grave of Staff Sergeant William "Glenn" Allen in the family plot in the Oconee Hills Cemetery in Athens, GA.
Below left: Grave of Staff Sergeant Richard Maculley in the American Cemetery at Margarten, the Netherlands.

Below right: No. 132, *Royal Flush*, over the target. Bomb bay doors are open and flak bursts around her.

the Service to return to Medford, Oregon, to become a manager for Modoc Orchards, where he had worked prior to enlisting. Sergeant Allen's body was returned to the Oconee Hills Cemetery in Athens, Georgia. Sergeant Maculley's remains were interred in the American Cemetery at Margarten, The Netherlands.

"*Mary Ruth*" *Memories of Mobile* would be a part of history, even if mainly as an unnoticed participant. Her first mission to Kiel, on 14 May, had been the longest and farthest of VIII Bomber Command to that date. The seventh, and last, mission would also be historic. This would be the first 'Maximum Effort' mission against the German fighter plane industry and the first 'Maximum Effort' daytime mission flown by VIII Bomber Command into the Ruhr Valley.

Unselfish dedication

The airmen associated with the "*Mary Ruth*" would typify the thousands of 'Black Jack' Pierces who worked frantically, often under almost impossible time and physical constraints, to repair and maintain 'their' planes so as to 'loan' them to the air crews for the next mission; the thousands of Ken Browns and Jim Quenins who wrestled their bomb-laden planes off runways and struggled to keep them in the air when hit by flak and

fighter cannon fire; the thousands of Vince Blileys who made certain the planes slipped into the proper places within their Elements as the formations came together, were on time and on course to the targets, and navigated them back to base when crippled by flak or fighters and had to leave their formations; the thousands of Jim Feericks who stared into the face of head-on attacking Luftwaffe fighters and listened to the clatter of flak tearing through the Alclad aluminium skin of the fuselage, while keeping a steady hand on the Norden bombsight to make certain the bombs were placed on the target; the thousands of Jim Akers, who kept the planes' flak-shattered equipment working, as well as manning the upper turret guns; the thousands of Bill Browns, Maurice Crains, and Ray Litzos who did their best to keep at bay the Me109 and FW190 fighters; and the thousands of Dick Maculleys and Glenn Allens who all too frequently died with their planes. As such, the crew of "*Mary Ruth*" *Memories of Mobile* epitomizes the unselfish dedication and ultimate sacrifices made by those who struggled to keep the planes flying and who flew and died in relative obscurity in the air over 'Fortress Europe' during the period of 1942–5.

The crews of *Memphis Belle*, of "*Mary Ruth*" *Memories of Mobile*, and the hundreds of other planes in VIII Bomber

JOE HARLICK

Command were not concerned about history that early Monday morning in East Anglia. Circumstances placed some of the planes and some of the crews more in the limelight of fame than others. The fate of many planes would be to be blown to bits at the end of runways whilst taking off, to be reduced to rubble in a farmer's field in Germany, to be entombed forever in the cold bottom waters of the North Sea, or to be incinerated into nothingness in a fiery ball over Berlin.

Other aircraft would survive, to end up in a field near Kingman, Arizona, Altus, Oklahoma, or Walnut Ridge, Arkansas. From there they would be converted into aluminium siding to build the Levittowns, into electric skillets, toasters, waffle irons, patio chairs, and the innumerable other consumer products needed to fulfil the postwar dreams of America. Sentimentalists may feel that to be an ignominious ending for planes who had endured so much. However, it was for the very fulfilment of those postwar dreams that they had risked the mid-air collisions whilst corkscrewing upward around the Buncher and Splasher homing beacons to assemble their formations in the crowded cloudy skies over East Anglia, had braved the box barrages of flak over St Nazaire and Merseburg, and had fought off the swarms of Me109s and FW190s on the way to Schweinfurt and Berlin. They had done their job and they had done it well. They would no longer be needed as instruments of war and were ready for realisation of the peace for which they had fought so valiantly.

Tail-end Charlie

Let us return once again to Bassingbourn and to "Mary Ruth" Memories of Mobile. Thirty six days have passed. The Lorient mission has been completed. All planes returned safely. Other missions have been flown and Memphis Belle and her crew have returned to the States.

It is another early morning in East Anglia. Today is Tuesday 22 June 1943, 0630 Double British Summer Time. Another mission is on, the Huls raid. "Mary Ruth" Memories of Mobile will be flying in the No. 3 position (rear outer left) of the last three-plane element of the echeloned left, Low Squadron of the Low Group, 'Tail-end Charlie'. The predawn flurry of ground crew activities has ceased and the crews are standing quietly beside their planes. The air crews are aboard, the pre-flight check lists completed. An apprehensive sombre silence lies over Bassingbourn.

Two green flares form an arch over the field. From dispersal points scattered about the base there comes an erratic chorus of sputtering coughs as planes come to life. Soon the ragged rumblings coalesce into a penetrating ear-rending roar as the multitude of engines are run up and additional instruments checked. Slowly the olive drab, graceful, deadly, low-winged fortresses begin moving down the taxiways in two weaving, snaking, nose to tail columns, brakes squealing, toward the end of the runway. The columns pause. Two flares arc upwards from Flying Control on the second story balcony outside the control room–green–green. The first B-17, No. 453, The Bearded Beauty – Mizpath, belches a cloud of blue smoke and rumbles down the 6,000-foot Runway 25, slowly struggling to clear the trees at the end. At 30-second intervals another follows, another, another, and yet another. No. 797, Old Ironsides, leaves on her journey to the bottom of the North Sea. No. 132, Royal Flush!, lifts off on her final flight. No. 998 (no name) tucks in her wheels one last time. No. 789, Golden Bear, heads for her long hibernation.

There is a hectic scramble around "Mary Ruth" Memories of Mobile. The No. 3 engine supercharger is not working. Sergeant Pierce clambers aboard and works rapidly. The pressure comes up seconds before an abort is declared. Brakes released, "Mary Ruth" jerks away from her hardstand, rolls along the taxiway, pivots, and lumbers quickly down runway No. 25. For the last time her wheels lift away from what later generations will refer to as the 'hallowed grounds' of East Anglia. "Mary Ruth" rises hurriedly and disappears into the distance as she heads for her nirvana and the obscurity of history. We watch her vanish with the confidence that those same later generations will say of "Mary Ruth" Memories of Mobile and of the others who will not return today, and all the days to come, 'We remember...we still remember.' ∎

Author information:
Lowell L. Getz, Professor Emeritus, Ecology, Ethology, and Evolution, University of Illinois, Urbana, IL 81801 and Colonel, Medical Service Corps, Retired.

Bravery on Instinct

Courage *n.* 1. the power or quality of dealing with or facing danger, fear, pain, etc.

Brave *adj.* 1. a. having or displaying courage, resolution, or daring; not cowardly or timid.

DOUG HUTCHINSON

As soon as I had finished the phone call with Australian air veteran Doug Hutchinson I pulled down my Collins English Dictionary. I needed to clarify a couple of words. In my opinion Doug's actions, modestly told, demonstrated that he had put these words to full use in saving the lives of his crewmates. But Doug claimed he simply had not thought like that at the time; he had acted on instinct.

In my opinion, Doug, whether instinctive or not, had acted extremely bravely and courageously. Would I have done the same?

I hope so!

Doug Hutchinson joined the Royal Australian Air Force in July 1940.

It was a time when Britain was at war and being a dominion we also entered the conflict with Germany. All my friends were starting to join the Army, as volunteers, and I began to think I should do something. I had tried to join the Air Force in 1938, before I was married, but they said I had missed the intake for that year and should apply again the following year. Well I got married and forgot about flying, then war broke out and I joined up.

Doug carried out his initial training, eight months, in his

homeland owing to his married status. After further training in Canada he was posted to the UK where he expressed an interest in Coastal Command and completed his operational training as a wireless operator, flying Bristol Blenheims. Doug was sent to the Middle East and No. 244 Squadron, operating over the Persian Gulf on naval co-operation, escort duties and anti-submarine patrols.

A period instructing in Kenya followed completion of his first tour. Doug was then sent back into 'action', to serve with No. 454 RAAF Squadron, then based at Gambut, Tobruk, flying Martin Baltimores on shipping strikes, anti-submarine work, and reconnaissance duties, although as Doug recalled, 'It was pretty mundane stuff', with regular entries of 'No sightings', and 'No incidents' recorded in the squadron diary. However, in July 1943 plans to deceive the enemy and draw opposing aircraft from the battle for Sicily would liven matters up.

On 23 July 1943 eight No. 454 Squadron Baltimores took part in Operation Thesis, or 'Black Friday' as it came to be known: an air assault on the Mediterranean island of Crete to divert pressure from the ongoing Allied invasion of Sicily. It is believed that planners confused the timings of the operation. The attack was scheduled for what was believed to be Cretan breakfast time, but the Allies were then on a different summer time basis to the islanders. Instead of being at the table, the German defenders were at their guns, waiting. No. 454 Squadron's eight aircraft were to attack in two waves of four bombers. At low level the Baltimores would grow large in sites of the anti-aircraft guns and the wreckage of five of these aircraft would be strewn over the island by the end of the day.

The task of No. 454 Squadron was to attack shipping in Souda Bay (sometimes spelt Suda Bay), on the north-west coast of Crete. Doug Hutchinson's usual navigator was sick with dysentery, and was replaced by Jasper Dyer.

There were two wireless operators/air gunners. We used to take it in turns, one in the top turret and one on the radio. On this particular day I happened to be in the turret. In the Baltimore everybody was separated from everybody else; you couldn't move about in the aircraft.

The distance to Crete was 230 miles, and we flew at sea level about 200 feet all the way. Two-thirds of the way across we were overtaken by the fighter squadrons, flying from other airfields. They went on ahead while we ploughed after them at an economical cruising speed.

Crete, a mountainous island, was visible long before we reached it, although we were flying low in the hope of escaping radar detection; probably pointless since the fighters would get there first and alert the defences.

Top: Doug in Kenya 1943.
Centre: Doug Hutchinson's steeds in action.
Bottom: Preparation for a raid.

Opposite page: The man himself in Canada, 1941.

Right: From left: Lionel Folkard RAF, Percy Willson RAF, and Doug Hutchinson RAAF.

Far right: Ken Wedgewood's resting place. One of 1,502 Commonwealth servicemen buried or commemorated at the Suda Bay War Cemetery.

We crossed the south coast near the eastern end of the island, which was less mountainous, and immediately the ground defences opened up on us, from underneath, from the sides, and from the front. We then had to climb over the central spine of the mountains, and at this time the defences scored their first hits.

Once over the mountains we came down to low-level again, and turned west along the coast to Souda Bay. We were now down to 100 feet and the fire was intense.

We had flown less than halfway to the target before we suffered serious damage. Our aircraft was the first to be hit, which was unusual since the formation leader is usually safest. It is the unfortunate aircraft bringing up the rear which generally suffer most.

The port engine burst into flames and every member of the crew was wounded. Lionel Folkard, the pilot, despite serious injury fought to control the aircraft.

Lionel was wounded in the left leg, and his right arm was hanging by a shred. He didn't have time to hesitate, and as he did not know if we were alive or dead he decided to put the aircraft down in a belly-landing on a narrow stretch of land near the beach.

This would be extremely difficult in the best of circumstances but Lionel only had the use of one arm, and blood was pooling on the floor of his cockpit. And if that was not enough the strip of beach they were heading for had been mined.

We left most of the explosions behind us as we skated over the ground, finally coming to rest. I had been in the turret for this trip and when it was evident we were to crash I threw the turret round to face forward and wrapped my arms around my face. The turret broke and somehow or other I was first out. I remember hanging by one finger on the side of the aircraft. I was wearing a ring which had caught on the edge of the aircraft and I was hanging a couple of feet off the ground. Finally the ring broke and I fell.

The fuselage had broken open, beneath the turret, and I reached in and dragged Ken Wedgewood through the gap, pulling him clear of the burning aircraft, but he appeared to be lifeless. I then turned my attention to the others, they were still conscious but in shock, and I could see Jasper in the nose of the plane bleeding profusely. The nose cone was broken and I helped him out and clear of the wreckage, which by this time was well on fire. I went to help Lionel, who was in a bad way, managing to get him clear just before the plane blew up; we had a full load of bombs. You just react without thinking. I had to get the others out. You just do it. It had to be done.

We then took stock of ourselves. We were in a mess. Wally had been badly hit in the forehead, Lionel seriously hit in the left leg and his right arm was nearly off. Just how Lionel landed the plane in his condition I will never know. I had a serious wound to my left foot and what was left of my boot was full of blood. I had also been hit in the left elbow and my back and face were burned and blackened.

A few minutes later we were confronted by a group of Italian

STEVE DARLOW

DOUG HUTCHINSON

Far left: Doug Hutchinson's POW identity card.
Centre: The signature of Doug Hutchinson, bottom right, inscribed in the POW logbook of Arthur Darlow. Both men were occupants of Stalag Luft III Belaria Compound, Block 6, Room 7.
Left: The man himself.

soldiers firing their guns over our heads. We immediately lifted our hands and began to walk towards them. To our surprise they turned and ran so we stopped and they stopped and started yelling and gesticulating. We immediately started walking again, and again they turned and ran, but this time we kept walking. It wasn't until a few minutes later that we realised we were walking through the minefield. Fortunately for us, we missed stepping on a mine.

The Italians then took us to a first aid station where our wounds were roughly dressed and we were driven in a van to the hospital at Heraklion. I was operated on by a German medical officer attended by Greek nurses, where the pieces of shrapnel and bullets were removed and my wounds dressed properly with paper bandages.

Here Doug was separated from his pilot and navigator. Doug was placed in a Junkers 52 that night on a stretcher, 'and one of the two guards was pointing a machine gun at me whilst the other shone a torch. It seemed ridiculous because I was unable to move.' Doug was taken to Athens, where he spent a day in a civilian prison cell, 'lousy with bugs, and between them and trying to reach the toilet, I was in great discomfort'. The following day he was entrained for Germany, 'each time the train stopped one of the guards would hop out and return with a cup of hot soup for me from the Red Cross stand at the station. When I wanted to urinate they gave me one of their helmets and tipped it out of the window.' On arrival in Frankfurt Doug was taken to 'what appeared to be a convalescent hospital where I was locked in a room on my own'.

I stayed in solitary confinement for about two weeks, and was daily interrogated by a German Luftwaffe Hauptmann, pressing questions about my unit, to which I only gave my rank and number. Then came the sexy woman interpreter who used her wiles to try and get information, with the same results as previously. By this time my wounds, which had not been re-dressed since my arrival, smelt to high heaven, and the Germans could take no more. I was despatched to Dulag Luft, where my very bloody bush-shirt was too much to bear and I was kindly given a British battle jacket so that I could wash the shirt. By this time I was hobbling around with a crutch and had one boot and my shorts.

After a day at Dulag Luft I was again taken to see an interrogation officer where the Hauptmann greeted me with, 'Right, if you won't tell us, we will tell you.' He then proceeded to read out where I lived, where I enlisted, when I joined, where I trained, where I had been since, details of my squadron, where we flew from, the numbers of each aircraft on the squadron and the type of aircraft.

Then he observed, 'For you the war is over.' I was never questioned again, and a day or two later we were loaded into trucks, taken to the railway, and placed in locked cattle trucks. Our destination was the POW camp at Sagan – Stalag Luft III.

Doug saw out the war behind wire, enduring the evacuation and forced march from Sagan to Luckenwalde in January 1945, and the frustrating wait after Russians liberated his prison camp – but that's another story. Doug, 91 at the time of writing, lives near Sydney, Australia. ∎

HEROES ALL
NOTRA J. BRIGHT · HENRY R. KRZYZAK · JOHN I. HOFFER

In February 1944 the father of American Eighth Air Force pilot Francis Flaherty, received news at his home in Prattsburg. His son had not returned from a mission over Germany. The families of Francis's crew, in their homes across the United States, had to deal with terrible uncertainty, receiving news they had always feared; co-pilot John Hoffer's father in Philipsburg, Pennsylvania; navigator Russell Austin's father in Electra, Texas; bombardier William Farrell's mother living in Waterbury, Connecticut; engineer/top turret gunner Notra Bright's mother in Lexington, Indiana; radio operator John Roe's mother in New York; ball turret gunner Burling Larson's mother in Buffalo, New York; right waist gunner Henry Krzyzak's mother living in Schenectady, New York; left waist gunner Casimer Bukowski's father in Buffalo, New York; and tail gunner Arthur Butler's brother from Washington DC. Six of these men – sons and brothers – were dead; the remaining four imprisoned.

Right: *The Mourning Woman* overlooking the Reflecting Pool at the Netherlands American Cemetery and Memorial.

Left: A grainy photograph of Francis Flaherty and his crew. Two of the men in the picture, Edward Doherty and Benjamin Saporta, would not be flying on the fateful 22 February 1944 mission. Back row (left to right): Notra Bright, Casimer Bukowski, Edward Doherty, Burling Larson, Henry Krzyzak, Arthur Butler. Front row (left to right): Francis Flaherty, John Hoffer, Benjamin Saporta, William Farrell.

At the end of the third week of February 1944 American bomber crews, based in England, were in the midst of what became known as 'Big Week', an all-out joint attack with the RAF against German aircraft production. RAF Bomber Command utilised the cover of darkness. The American Eighth Air Force dared the Luftwaffe to oppose their formations of bombers, bristling with guns, in the daylight hours.

On 20 February 'Big Week' opened for the Eighth Air Force, with just over 1,000 American heavy bombers, escorted by 835 fighters, taking off from their English bases; 21 of these heavies would not be returning home that evening. On the following day 16 of the 861 bombers despatched to continue the attack would be recorded as missing. On 22 February the Eighth Air Force maintained the assault, with 799 bombers despatched. Poor weather seriously hampered the effectiveness of the mission in terms of the objectives. It also seriously

disrupted the abilities of the crews to assemble into their combat formations over England, from which the crews were to fly due east to the target area, a long flight through hostile airspace. On this day fierce opposition was expected. Expectations were met and the Eighth Air Force's 381st Bomb Group would be in the midst of the action.

In James Good Brown's account of his time as Chaplain with the 381st Bomb Group he vividly recalled the after-effects of the 22 February mission.

Long will I remember the look on the faces of the men who returned from the raid on Bunde, Germany…everything the Germans had, opened against our fliers. All hell broke loose. The men who returned from Bunde described what took place, but their description was nothing compared with the look on their faces. Some looked wild. Others looked weird. Others looked haggard and worn out. Others looked disappointed. Others cried because of what they saw

happening to our men. Others were almost hysterical and talked fast. Others were sick – physically sick. The strain was too much for them.

John W. Howland, a navigator with the 381st Bomb Group, recorded his thoughts on the mission in his diary.

Up at 0500 again and briefed for Oschersleben–Bunde. I didn't feel right about this mission and wasn't too enthused about going. However, we took off as scheduled and climbed to 11,000 ft to assemble. Metro said it would be clear at that altitude. We found it was quite hazy, and had dense, persistent contrails. We looked and looked, but couldn't find our Group. Finally, at Group departure time and location, we tacked onto Major Fitzgerald and started out with 4 or 5 other ships. A few minutes later, we picked up the 91st Bomb Group (triangle A); but we still couldn't find the 381st Bomb Group (triangle L).

Over Clacton, we made a 360-degree turn to the left and found our element

**CREW LOST ON 22/02/1944
BOEING B-17G, VE–M,
SERIAL NUMBER: 42-31443,
NAME: 'FRIDAY THE 13TH'
532ND SQUADRON, 381ST
BOMB GROUP**

Pilot: Lieutenant
Francis J. Flaherty   KIA

Co-pilot: 2nd Lieutenant
John I. Hoffer   KIA

Navigator: Flying Officer
Russell D. Austin   POW

Bombardier: 2nd Lieutenant
William R. Farrell   POW

Eng./Top Turret Gunner:
Tech. Sergeant Notra J. Bright **KIA**

Radio Operator:
Tech. Sergeant John P. Roe   POW

Ball Turret Gunner:
Staff Sergeant Burling Larson **KIA**

Left Waist Gunner: Staff Sergeant
Casimer L. Bukowski   POW

Right Waist Gunner: Staff Sergeant
Henry R. Krzyzak   KIA

Tail Gunner: Staff Sergeant
Arthur N. Butler   KIA

leader, Meyers. We flew his right wing as we were supposed to. Then, we saw Major Fitzgerald and about four other 381st planes fly off, but Meyers kept circling. We stayed with our element leader. Finally we decided things were SNAFU [Situation Normal All F****d Up], and went back to base. We had 'booby trap' 500lb demolition bombs on board. The tower instructed us to fly out over the North Sea and drop them. After returning, we found that we weren't the only ones to get screwed up in assembly. All but nine of the entire 381st Bomb Group had returned to base.

We waited for our nine ships to return. Like the infamous raid carried out to Oschersleben on January 11th, today's raid was another slaughter. Only 3 of the nine ships returned.

The 381st Bomb Group's 535th Squadron diary provides a good summary of the mission that day.

Today the group learned the true meaning of tight formation, large numbers of bombers and a full fighter escort. Thirty-one Forts took off this morning but some of the filthiest weather conditions over not a high altitude prevented the majority of them from bombing. Nineteen of them aborted, three of them out of the six sent by this squadron.

Twelve, including Lts Smith, Hustedt and Downey followed Major John Fitzgerald of the 532nd, to a rendezvous with 15 Forts from the 91st BG. These 27 ships, late for their escort, proceeded over the German coast alone, headed for Aschersleben [also referred to as Oschersleben in many narratives]. About an hour inside Germany they were hit by more than 200 German fighters of high calibre. Major Fitzgerald had two sets of wingmen shot down. The group lost six, three from the 535th. The target bombed was Bunde, after more than 40 minutes of constant attack from enemy fighters, mostly FW190s.

One of the six crews that had been in the midst of the air fight was the aircraft of Lieutenant Francis J. Flaherty. The Missing Air Crew Report for the Flaherty crew gives some insight into what happened inside their aircraft that day when they met the 'high calibre' German fighters. Questionnaires filled out by surviving crew members, on their return from prison camp, although brief, do try and explain the fate of their colleagues.

Following an attack by fighters, which mortally damaged his B-17, Francis Flaherty quickly made the decision to abandon the aircraft. John Roe, the radio operator, recalled seeing

Right: 'Friday the 13th' Serial number 42-31443, in the foreground on a mission to Germany prior to the fateful raid on 22 February 1944.

NETHERLANDS AMERICAN CEMETERY

NOTRA J. BRIGHT
Technical Sergeant, 532nd Bomber
Squadron, 381st Bomber Group, Heavy
Died: 22 February 44
Buried at: Plot P, Row 22, Grave 15
Awards: Air Medal with 2 Oak Leaf
Clusters, Purple Heart

JOHN I. HOFFER
Second Lieutenant, 532nd Bomber
Squadron, 381st Bomber Group, Heavy
Died: 22 February 44
Buried at: Plot C, Row 18, Grave 20
Awards: Air Medal with Oak Leaf
Cluster

HENRY R. KRZYZAK
Staff Sergeant, 532nd Bomber
Squadron, 381st Bomber Group, Heavy
Died: 22 February 44
Buried at: Plot M, Row 22, Grave 13
Awards: Air Medal with Oak Leaf
Cluster, Purple Heart

Left: The Netherlands
American Cemetery.
Below left: John Roe's
MACR questionnaire
recalling John Hoffer's
cry to his crewmates
to get out.

his skipper Flaherty signal with his hands to get out and John Hoffer, the co-pilot, yelling 'Get Out.' Roe then recalled, 'As soon as I left the pilot's comp some shells exploded hitting the oxygen tanks causing the plane to burn rapidly.' Roe managed to bale out, suffering from shrapnel wounds to his left side.

One survivor (it is not clear who) believed tail gunner Arthur Butler, 'got it on the first pass, as nothing was heard from him during or after said attack'. Burling Larson, the ball turret gunner, was standing with left waist gunner Casimer Bukowski when a 20mm shell burst and Larson fell, doubled up. Bukowski was not unscathed, 'I think he was killed with the same bursts that wounded me.'

It was later surmised that the other waist gunner, Henry R. Krzyzak, was also killed near his weapon by 20mm fire from enemy fighters. One survivor (possibly Roe or Bukowski) stated he checked him before he jumped.

Notra Bright was last seen in the top turret by John Roe, and it was believed he was killed in the aircraft. Bukowski's questionnaire records that he thought John Hoffer had managed to bale out and evade capture, but it would seem that Hoffer had gone down with the aircraft.

The B-17 plummeted down, coming to earth at Brake-Senne near Bielefeld at 1340 hours. Six of the crew were killed.

James Good Brown, in the account of his time as Chaplain with the Bomb Group, summarised the feeling of loss.

We feel sorry for the men who were shot down on the Bunde raid of February 22, 1944. Our hearts are deeply grieved for the many men who were killed. And we pity those who saw what happened to their comrades who were shot down. They had not only the agony of facing death with little hope of survival themselves, but endured the sight of their fellow fliers going down one after another.

General George Washington, Commander-in-Chief of the Colonial Army, would be proud of these 60 American patriots who went down in combat today. Were General George Washington here today, he would call them THE MIGHTY MEN OF THE 381st.

All six of the men killed on 'Friday the 13th' were initially buried at Senne Cemetery. Post-war three were transferred to the Netherlands American Cemetery. At the request of the other three men's next-of-kin, their bodies were returned to the USA. ■

The Netherlands American Cemetery is located in the village of Margraten, 6 miles east of Maastricht, on the main road to Aachen, Germany. Further cemetery details can be found via the following website:
http://www.abmc.gov/cemeteries/ne.php

Sources: James Good Brown's *The Mighty Men of the 381st: Heroes All* (www.381st.org). Thanks to the American Battle Monuments Commission, Sell Martha, Arthur Brookes, Thomas Culbert, John Howland, Bill Haggerty, Joe Waddell, and Dr James Good Brown (106 years old!).

Into Enemy Arms

As I sat with Eighth Air Force veteran pilot Harry Selling, it was clear that he was recalling extremely moving memories. Whilst listening I was trying to visualise Harry's experiences. But Harry had those images firmly fixed in his mind. They are memories and sights he has never been able to forget.

B-17 Flying Fortress pilot Harry Selling arrived at Glatton, Huntingdonshire, England, home of the USAAF Eighth Air Force's 457th Bomb Group, in the middle of June 1944. Airmen of the 'Mighty Eighth' had been fighting the daylight air battle in Europe for nearly two years, the American heavy bomber force having developed to such an extent that on the first mission of D-Day itself 1,805 bombers had taken off from their English bases to support the Allied assault on the Normandy beaches. But the Luftwaffe had exacted its toll in the preceding months; thousands of American airmen had already lost their lives, and thousands more were in captivity. It was therefore not surprising that 'old' hands at a bomb group showed some indifference to new arrivals. What was the point of establishing a relationship when the raw recruit may only last a few missions?

On arrival at Glatton', recalls Harry, 'I bought a bicycle and checked in to where I was going to live. There was one other crew in my hut; but very little exchange or conversation. No, "How's it going?", or anything like that. I just became one of the Group.

My first mission, on 14 August, involved flying with an experienced crew. I got to the briefing, it was very smoky, and I was trying to keep my emotions all under control, I was just a

spectator. They released the blind over the map and we were going to Stuttgart, a well-guarded target. Lots of hooping and groaning and then the CO, Colonel Luper, entered the back of the auditorium, he was a West Pointer. He got up on stage and said, "At ease men, everything's OK men." He had a riding crop under his arm and he was right out of Hollywood, central casting, a showman. He sat down and someone else took over telling us the details of what was going to happen this day. I'm there with all my new stuff, everything I had was brand new. I'm in my woolly clothes, I didn't have an electric suit, I had fleece-lined stuff, and that's a lot of stuff. I got myself a jeep and driver and noticed that I was to fly with a Captain.

I got out to the hardstand, it was all foggy, and I walked up to the Captain, saluted and said, "Reporting for duty sir", right out of the book. He looked me up and down and took me around to each member of the crew and introduced me. There was no eye contact, just a "Hi, how's it going?" We met each crew member and finally he took me aside, looked at me and said "Are you going to wear that gun?" I had the gun in a holster tied with a thong. I said, "Yeh." He said, "Have you filed the sights off it yet?" I said "No. Should I?" He said, "Yes, so that when they shove it up your arse it won't hurt." He told me to take the gun off and sit on it. So here I was ready for war and he doesn't want me that ready.

Top: Harry Selling, December 1942, as a training cadet.

Faded photos from Harry's collection.
Clockwise from top: Harry Selling, Pilot; Navigator Lieutenant Robert F. Marcum; Bombardier Lieutenant Howard L. Peterson in front of B-17 'American Eagle'; Waist gunner Sergeant Stephen V. Gallucci; Aircraft Engineer Sergeant James P. Shadman; Radio Operator Sergeant Edwin C. Krueger (left), and Aircraft Engineer Sergeant James P. Shadman (right).

PLANE s/n 42-31383
12 September 1944

Pilot:
Lt Harry H. Selling

Co-pilot:
Lt Lloyd D. French

Navigator:
Lt Robert F. Marcum

Bombardier:
Lt Howard L. Peterson

Aircraft Engineer:
Sgt James P. Shadman

Radio Operator:
Sgt Edwin C. Krueger

Left Waist Gunner:
Sgt Donald W. Conley

Ball Turret Gunner:
Sgt Stephen V. Gallucci

Tail Gunner:
Sgt Leo A. Ryder

HARRY SELLING

Right: Harry Selling demonstrates his gymnastic skills at Avon Park Florida, April 1944.

We climbed into the plane and were getting ready to start the engines. I picked up the check list and when I started reading it the Captain took it out of my hand and said, "What do you want that for", and he threw it behind us, just got rid of it, saying, "We don't need that." We started the engines, taxied out, and took off and he's doing all the manoeuvrings. We flew up through the fog to about 8,000 feet, and saw the flares, so we knew which Group to form on. We were all milling around and finally got into our position. We were going to fly with 36 ships this day, it took at

"They came and shook my hand and said 'You can fly with us anytime.' I hadn't panicked. I hadn't been an embarrassment"

least 40 minutes to get everybody airborne, so a lot of waiting to get everybody together to form the stream going to the target. The Captain put us into formation and then said, "Now don't run into anything. You fly." We started going east, nearly 1,200 bombers, although not all going to the same place, each had a particular target. It was a bright sunny day at this altitude. I was under no stress except to fly, nobody was shooting at us.

The minute we got to the coast the occasional puff of flak

appeared. Suddenly I realised that we were in war and they were trying to kill me. But I'm still doing what I'm doing. I'm not anxious, it's still a lark. But then it got more and more dense and the plane started to feel it, things were hitting us. We carried out oxygen checks and there were no injuries. Pretty soon the Captain said, "I'll take over." He started flying the plane from the Initial Point and then the bombardier took over. We were on that bomb run for at least 10 minutes, with lots of flak. I had no fear, I didn't know what to be afraid of. I knew that there were bullets, but I wasn't thinking "Oh my God." Suddenly it was "bombs away", and you can't imagine what a wonderful sound that was. We're going home, we're going to get the hell out of here. We did a 180 and started back and as the distance increased there was less and less defence. It was over then for us, we were trying to get the hell out of there.

We got back to the base, about 4.30 p.m. and landed without incident, the tyres were still inflated. The whole tone of everything had changed and I was one of them. They came and shook my hand and said, "You can fly with us anytime." I hadn't panicked, I hadn't been an embarrassment. I didn't do anything I shouldn't have done. I was now one of the team. Then I went back to my barracks and told everyone about what we had experienced. We had a lot of damage, there were over 50 holes, and it was amazing that no one got hurt.

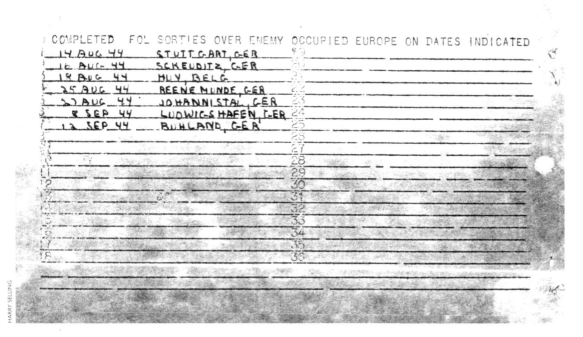

COMPLETED FOL SORTIES OVER ENEMY OCCUPIED EUROPE ON DATES INDICATED

14 AUG 44	STUTTGART, GER	
16 AUG 44	SCKEUDITZ, GER	
18 AUG 44	HUY, BELG	
25 AUG 44	REENE MUNDE, GER	
27 AUG 44	JOHANNISTAL, GER	
8 SEP 44	LUDWIGSHAFEN, GER	
12 SEP 44	RUHLAND, GER	

Left: Harry Selling's mission listing.

Two days later, Harry took his own crew to Germany and over the course of the next four weeks he took his mission tally to six. Flak had been the main opposition and he had been fortunate that to date there had been no contact with enemy fighters. On his seventh mission to Ruhland, however, his B-17 would appear in the sights of an enemy fighter.

Harry recalls that he and his fellow bomber airmen were sent on the 12 September mission to provoke the Luftwaffe into a fight.

It was a challenge — let's have it out! The target we had was Ruhland. We were going by the way of Berlin, with the target further south. It was uneventful until we got to Berlin, and then my navigator said, "Harry, look over to your left." I looked and we were on a collision course with another group of planes. We were going to shuffle the deck; everybody was trying to avoid collision.

Eight combat wings of the 1st Division had been sent to attack oil targets in the vicinity of Ruhland. The 36-ship formation of the 457th Bomb Group, took its place in the 94th A Combat Wing. After crossing the North Sea, and the enemy coast, the formation flew to a position

north-east of Berlin, then turned south toward the Initial Point. Behind the 457th Bomb Group, another Group was positioned at a higher altitude, but was lagging behind because of a difference in wind speed. When they turned near Berlin they experienced heavy flak, which they sought to avoid by turning again. In doing so, the low box of their formation 'shuffled' through the high box of the 457th Bomb Group. In the confusion some Luftwaffe pilots seized their chance.

I dumped the controls so they missed us, which was a miracle, and just then I heard my upper turret guns firing right behind me, and I hadn't heard those firing before. I looked back to see what he was firing at and it was a Focke-Wulf 190, coming in at 7 o'clock, maybe a 100 yards behind, firing 20mm cannon. The shells burst in through the window and struck the instrument panel, wrecking the whole thing, just tore it up. I was amazed I wasn't getting hit. The back of my seat was armour plated so I don't know if any shells hit there. Then the column hit me on the chest and we went into a vertical climb until the aircraft stalled. When you are in an unusual position like that the people that are not strapped in, they fall, the waist gunners are tumbling down to the tail. The ball turret gunner is OK but the navigator and the bombardier are loose, not strapped in, and they get banged around. After this

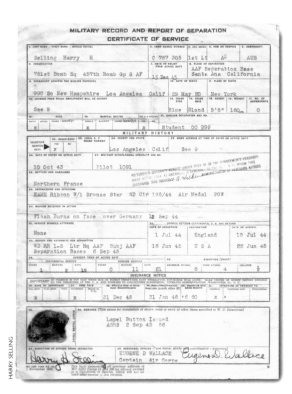

vertical climb the aircraft did a hammerhead stall and started
spinning. A fire broke out in the cockpit and my co-pilot, getting
up to go down through the hatch, was consumed by the fire. By
this time I had taken my mask off and I got my face all burned.
My co-pilot died right there in front of me, it was over in an
instant. I sat back in my chair and I thought, "I guess this is it",
but I felt guilty, what a waste, I had only been on 7 missions. All
my training was for nothing and I hadn't contributed enough.

At those speeds and falling, even within the plane, you get
really disorientated and banged up. There is no way the rest of the
crew could have survived because of the gyration.

With his aircraft on fire and breaking up, Harry lost
consciousness.

When I awakened, it was quiet except for the wind noise. I
discovered that I was up on the instrument panel, on my back and
my feet were to the right window. I tried to kick it open but I
couldn't budge it. When I got to where the window lock was I
noticed that the rest of the plane was gone and I was just in a little
piece of it. I looked down, the seats were gone. The upper turret ring
was there but the rest was just broken up into small pieces of
plane. So I just rolled out. The cushion which I sat on was my back
pack, so I didn't have to look for anything. The rest of the crew have
a harness and a chest pack which they put somewhere handy, and

they snap it on when they need it. The fact that I didn't have to
look for anything was obviously very good. The chute opened, at
about 800 feet, and trees were visible. I started to prepare myself
for parachute control then I went into the trees. I hit a bull's-eye,
the canopy caught on the foliage and I had a wonderful landing
without shock. I shimmied down the tree and apart from the burns
to my face I was without injury.

I started running north, for maybe 20 minutes, finally stopping
and climbing a tree, where I went through my papers and the stuff
that I had, which I destroyed. Then I looked at the maps I had of
France and Germany, wonderful silk maps. It was about 2 o'clock
and I was so exhausted so I decided to take a nap, for about an hour.

When I awoke I moved off and saw a woman planting
potatoes; we had been instructed to contact a civilian in this
situation. As I was creeping up on her, two kids were suddenly
standing over me. I looked up and said, "Hi guys." They seemed so
friendly and I felt they were going to help me. They were talking
about a cellar so I went with them. They took me right to the
Wehrmacht. We were in a village and I was extremely tired, with
the shock and everything else, and I was just trying to keep
myself together. I kept sitting down and then crowds started
gathering. They were clearly thinking "Here's the guy who has been
giving us sleepless nights and sleepless days." Here I was, the
enemy, and they had finally got one of us. They started abusing me,
it was mostly soldiers, and kicking me, and it started to build as

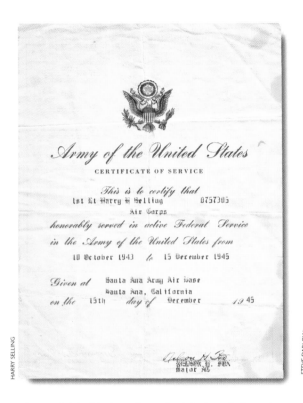

other people joined in, it was becoming infectious. At that point when I was really very concerned about my future, this old man, from the Wehrmacht, came over with a gun, fired it and told them to leave me alone. He led me away and walked me to a Luftwaffe base, about 3 miles away. We talked and he told me he had one son on the western front and one on the eastern front. He kept telling me that he was so happy for me, "For you the war is over." It was so wonderful. When we parted we embraced. I was no threat to him and I think he saw his son in me. He wished that both of them were on the western front.

Harry now had to come to terms with life as a prisoner of war, as he was 'processed' and interrogated in transit camps, which had swelled considerably in line with the escalation of the bomber offensive.

There were so many of us and there was really nothing personal about anything, they had to keep us all moving. At interrogation, at the transit camp at Wetzlar, this man was so friendly; he threw me a Hershey bar. I kept giving name, rank and number but they knew a lot more, they had my aeroplane. At one point he said, "Harry, come here, I want to show you something." He started going through this big scrapbook, showing details about the Groups, the COs, locations. He got to the 457th but didn't stop and went three pages further. Then he said, "Oh Harry, I'm sorry, you were in the

457th." He went back and looked at me and said, "How's old 360 Luper?" That was his nickname because he used to get on target and if it wasn't perfect he said let's go around. It really was interesting that they had so much information.

From Wetzlar we went to a staging area before we went to Stalag Luft I, Barth, to get clothes and a great coat, everything you needed to survive a winter. We were entrained and had to go through Frankfurt, but we couldn't go through to get on the next train because of the rubble. That area was always bombed, they would fix it and we would bomb it. So we were detrained and armed guards with dogs escorted us, about 30 to 40 guys, into the main part of the station. There were two ladies serving potato soup. I hadn't eaten so I was really hungry. This lady came over and asked me if I would like some potato soup. I wolfed it down and she said "Would you like another?" When she said that I started crying. I couldn't handle this kindness from the enemy, it just got to me. She took me in her arms and held me; the enemy was embracing me. It was such a tender moment. It was right from heaven really, it was such a loving act. That soup was so wonderful.

Harry saw out the war at Stalag Luft I, eventually returning to his homeland, weighing considerably less than when he first left. But he has never forgotten the gesture of kindness shown to him by the enemy amidst the rubble in Frankfurt. 'I've liked potato soup ever since.' ∎

Screaming for Help

On 24 April 1944, deep over Germany, a USAAF 355th Fighter Group Mustang pilot received word that his compatriots, flying their Eighth Air Force heavy bombers, were under attack, and they were 'screaming for help'. Robert E. Woody immediately went to their assistance. It was not long before the enemy was in his sights. At the end of the day Woody had become an 'Ace'.

AIRCRAFT ILLUSTRATIONS: PETE WEST

In the first half of 1944 the American Eighth Air Force put the Luftwaffe on the defensive. It was a significant strategic turning point in the air battle. Deep bomber penetrations into Reich airspace forced the Luftwaffe to withdraw fighter aircraft from other battle fronts. Accompanying the American four-engine heavy bombers was their 'Little Friends', the long-range fighter pilots. It became a battle of attrition. History now shows that the Allies could cope, but the Luftwaffe could not. American fighter pilots like Robert E. Woody fought the fierce and violent air battle over Germany. They ensured that in subsequent campaigns, such as the D-Day landings and the battle for Normandy, they were responsible for the all - important local air superiority.

On 24 April the Eighth Air Force despatched 754 bomb-laden B-17s and B-24s to industrial and airfield targets in the Munich, Friedrichshafen, and Gablingen/Leipheim areas. It was a deep penetration, with fighter support provided by the Eighth's Fighter Command, and the RAF and US Ninth Air Forces. More fighters than bombers were involved in the mission, although only the Eighth's pilots would be able to take their long-range aircraft to the target area.

Post-raid analysis recorded 716 bombers effective, and 40 MIA, 27 of these lost from the 1st Bomb Division attack on the Landsberg, Oberpfaffenhofen, and Erding targets around Munich. As the bombers neared the target area the German fighter force, out in strength, engaged the bombers. Where was the escort? Frantically, calls were made for help. Pilots of the 355th Fighter Group heard and came. ■

Below left:
Mustang Ace Captain Robert E. Woody.

ENCOUNTER REPORT

A. COMBAT
B. B. 24 April 1944
C. 354TH FIGHTER SQUADRON, 355TH FIGHTER GROUP, AAF STATION F-122, APO 637, U.S. ARMY
D. ABOUT 1345
E. SOUTHEAST OF MUNICH NEAR ROGOERSDORF
F. CAVU
G. COMBAT WITH 5 ME109S
H. 4 ME109S - DESTROYED, 1 ME109 - DESTROYED, SHARED WITH LT. BOULET, 1 ME109 - DAMAGED

I was leading Yellow Flight. We made R/V with the bombers at about 1335 and were flying at about 23,000 feet with the main box of B/F. About 10 minutes later Yellow 2 received a call from a box of bombers and reported they were screaming for help. Yellow 3 then called and said that a small box of B/F was being attacked about 3 o'clock to us. We immediately turned toward this box under attack.

While we were still some distance from the bombers I saw one of them explode and go down so I gave my ship full throttle and in the process of catching up with the bombers I looked around to size up the situation. I observed 15 or 20 contrails at about 28,000 feet, 5,000 feet above us and I also saw approximately 8 e/a going through the bomber formation. As we were drawing closer I saw a second bomber go spiralling down with about 4 or 5 chutes popping out behind him. I was getting mad as hell at the Jerries by this time.

We were approaching the bombers from about 9 o'clock at their level and were just about 3,000 yards away from them when I saw one lone e/a playing around near the rear of the bombers. I also saw five more e/a which I identified as Me109s at 1 o'clock to me making a pass from 8 o'clock to the bombers in line abreast formation with the leader evidently slightly ahead and to the left so I made a slight left turn and came about behind 'tail end charlie' who was furthest on the right. I waited until I was about 300 yards dead astern of him before I opened fire. I gave him a good burst and saw my strikes immediately all over his fuselage and wing root. The e/a began pouring out black smoke, shuddered as he was hit by the concentration of my fire and fell off on his left wing going almost straight down and burning. I CLAIM THIS E/A DESTROYED.

Far left:
Crew Chief Staff Sergeant Gertzen maintaining Captain Robert E "The Kid" Woody's P-51B 43-6520 WR-W 'Woody's Maytag'.
Left: Crew Chief Staff Sergeant Gertzen and Captain Robert E "The Kid" Woody seem satisfied with the performance of Woody's Maytag, April 1944.

I had expected the other four e/a to break as soon as I shot their 'tail end charlie' down but they evidently were intent on getting the bombers and didn't notice my attack so I moved up on the next e/a. We were now about 1,200 yards from the bombers and I knew the bombers would shoot at me if I followed the e/a through their formation but that was a chance I had to take. I quickly squared away dead astern of him about 275 yards away and gave him a good burst. My hits around the fuselage and wing roots just about tore the e/a apart. He too shook violently then began pouring dense black smoke and the a/c lazily fell off on its left wing and slowly fell off going into a spin.

There was no question in my mind but that my guns were well bore-sighted and that I was hitting with all four guns. It may be boastful to say but I honestly believe that this pilot was definitely killed instantly as was the one I mentioned above and the others to follow. I CLAIM THIS E/A DESTROYED.

I lined up on the third e/a. By this time I had gradually closed to about 250 yards and my burst, again from dead astern hit in exactly the same spots as the two prior e/a. I saw a lot of small pieces fall off the e/a from around his cockpit and it began spewing coolant and the black smoke again began to pour both from the cockpit and all around the fuselage. He fell off and went spinning down. I CLAIM THIS E/A DESTROYED.

By this time we were only about 800 yards from the bombers and the high contrails had disappeared so I began to worry a little. I quickly slid in behind No.4

Right: Captain Robert E. Woody and 'Woody's Maytag' crew, April 1944.
Far right: 355th Fighter Group Memorial – Steeple Morden.

and opened up on him from dead astern and a range of approximately 225 yards. This one also lit up like a Christmas tree with parts flying off. His coolant shot back all around me and in the midst of it I could see the dense black smoke. He went spinning down also. I CLAIM THIS E/A DESTROYED.

I pulled up about 200 yards behind the sole remaining e/a, again got the bead on him and observed strikes concentrated in the fuselage and wing roots. Black smoke, oil and coolant poured out, his oil covering my windscreen and canopy. The e/a went straight down and undoubtedly the pilot never knew what happened to him. Before I had fired at this e/a Lt. Boulet, my wingman, had lined him up and according to his own report given it a good burst.**

After shooting down these five e/a I made a turn to get away from the bombers and I then spotted a lone Me109 coming in from about 10 o'clock at the same level. I

turned into him and he started down in a spiral. I turned on the inside of him and gave him a short burst with good deflection, seeing my hits strike on his wings and fuselage but I ran out of ammunition, Damnit. The e/a then rolled over and hit for the deck. I CLAIM THIS E/A AS DAMAGED.

I pulled up to reform my flight, calling my No. 3 man, Lt. Fortier, to take over. He took over the flight and I fell into No. 4 position. I saw him go after an Me109 on the deck firing at it from about 300 yards. I saw this Me109 crash in flames.

Several other 109s appeared but as I was out of ammunition I felt I would be more of a liability than an asset to the flight - all I did was keep turning into the e/a and causing them to break and hit the deck.

I have done a lot of skeet shooting but never did I see clay pigeons put on a better exhibition than these 109s.

Robert E. Woody. Capt, Air Corps

** I CLAIM THIS ME109 - DESTROYED - SHARED WITH LT. BOULET

ℹ With thanks to Bill Marshall, Peter Randall, Mike Williams, and Neil Stirling.

WE GAVE OUR TODAY
ALLAN JOHN HANCOCK · IDWAL JAMES DAVIES

Right:
Commonwealth
War Graves
Cemetery, Bayeux.

Allied pilots involved in ground-attack operations during the Normandy campaign in 1944 will never forget the intense flak. Although the Allies held and utilised air superiority over the battlefield, the danger from the guns on the ground was ever present. When the shell fired from a flak gun tore through a Typhoon wing, or a Mustang engine, or a Thunderbolt cockpit, there was little if any time for the pilot to either try and make a forced landing or rapidly exit his dying steed. Flak claimed many airmen's lives over Normandy.

In the run-up to the 6 June 1944 D-Day assault on the Normandy beaches, the rate of Allied fighter-bomber sorties escalated. In particular a campaign against enemy coastal radar stations was attempted to blind the Germans to the Channel crossing. But these operations could be costly, as experienced by No. 198 Squadron, flying Typhoons, on 2 June 1944, when they suffered 'quite a blow', losing their CO. Leading an attack on radar installations at Dieppe, Squadron Leader J. Niblett DFC was hit by light flak; his aircraft 'burst into a mass of flames and crashed into the cliffs'. A replacement was quickly found, the No. 198 Squadron diary recording on 3 June: 'Good news greeted us late this evening for we have just heard that our new C.O. is from our fellow Wing Squadron (No. 609 Sqn) S/Ldr I.J. Davies DFC who takes over Command immediately.'

Old hands

Idwal James 'Dave' Davies took up his new responsibilities when the UK based RAF fighter squadrons were making final preparations to support the imminent seaborne assault. Idwal Davies was one of many RAF airmen who had gained valuable fighting experience in the preceding months and years. Indeed, many 'old hands', which men in their twenties were called then, brought their experience to bear in the forthcoming challenge.

After spending time instructing in the Middle East earlier in the war, Idwal Davies returned to the UK, and following a spell at an operational training unit joined No. 609 Squadron at Manston on 6 April 1943. On 1 June 1943, flying a Typhoon Ib he was involved in the interception of FW190s, which were carrying out a low-level attack on Margate and Broadstairs in Kent, claiming 3 shot down. A spell at No. 137 Squadron

CHRIS THOMAS

CHRIS GOSS

Top: A.J. Hancock.
Below: I.J. Davies.

on Hurricanes, as a flight commander, followed in the autumn, and then he was posted back to No. 609 as flight commander of 'A' Flight. On 4 January 1944, during an attack on Gilze-Rijen, Davies claimed a Dornier 217 and a share of 3 aircraft on the ground.

Another of the 'old hands' preparing for the support to the invasion was No. 129 Squadron's Allan John Hancock, having learnt his trade supporting the Army in North Africa. John Hancock was certainly more than a capable pilot. His 'Above Average' gradings during training hinted at his potential, and whilst

flying operationally with No. 80 and then No. 213 Squadrons over North Africa and Syria, in 1941/2, he fulfilled expectations. Chris Shores and Clive Williams', *Aces High* records 4 destroyed, 1 shared, and 3 probables in the air, and 2 destroyed and 6 damaged on the ground. Hancock's first tour came to a conclusion when he was wounded on 10 June 1942, but reward for his efforts would come with a DFC. In March 1943 he took up combat flying again with No.64 Squadron in the UK, and in September 1943 he joined No. 129 Squadron as a flight commander, with further success aerial: two damaged

and one destroyed. On D-Day itself, flying a Mustang III, he would add to his tally. Davies would also fly on 6 June and quite probably both men, like their squadron colleagues, knew that they were about to be involved in one of the most important events of the entire war.

Day of days

On the eve of D-Day the No. 129 Squadron diarist summed up the sense of anticipation: '...at 23.15 hours, the Squadron was briefed on its role in the forthcoming invasion. The Squadron is naturally on tenterhooks at the prospect of finally coming to grips with the Hun.' But early the next day frustration set in.

'A very big reaction set in temporarily today when it was known that although at long last THE DAY had arrived, the Fighting Hundred and Twenty-ninth Pursuit were only participating as a reserve squadron. Bickering between pilots was prevalent but gave place to joyous celebrations when it was known that we were to carry out a show in the evening. The Squadron, led by the Wing Commander, escorted gliders and their tugs to the Beachhead. The day was perfected by the announcement that F/Lt. Hancock and W/C. Rigby, flying Blue 1 and 2 respectively, destroyed a FW190 – the Squadron's first victim on Mustangs. The beach scene, it was felt, would long be remembered by all lucky enough to see it.'

"Clobbering" the enemy

No. 198 Squadron Typhoon pilots also made their contribution to D-Day, carrying out a rocket attack on a Chateau near St Lô. 'Many hits on the building were seen and as the last a/c left the scene of the attack fire and smoke was issuing from ground floor windows of the Chateau. Pilots

Right: A fine pencil sketch of Flight Lieutenant Idwal Davies DFC, whilst with No. 609 Squadron.

F/L' I.J.DAVIES. DFC

609 SQUADRON

VIA MARK CRAME

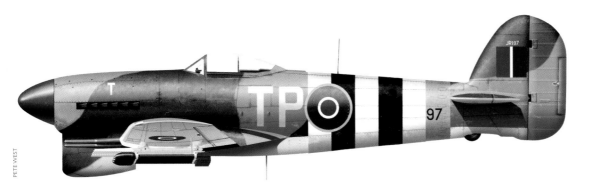

PETE WEST

reported having seen tremendous activity just off the beaches as one of our members so aptly remarked "there were more ships than sea".

Over the course of the next few days No. 129 Squadron was certainly in the thick of it, the squadron ORB records numerous attacks on enemy transport: 7 June, 'Bombing was above average and the strafing after was excellent, approximately 30 vehicles being "clobbered" to mean tune', 8 June, '...at 14.15, four aircraft led by F/Lt. Hancock took off for the same area [Falaise], this time without bombs, and after rather a long while in the area, which was covered with extremely bad weather, had their patience rewarded by strafing a staff car, and a motorcyclist, writing off, and by setting on fire, a Mark IV Tank. This tank, in company with others, stopped, and the crews, disembarking from them were immediately "squirted" by all four aircraft with

deadly effect.' The No. 129 Squadron pilots were certainly utilising the local air superiority, but ground fire was ever present and on 10 June 'two of the older hands on the squadron' failed to return, the Mustangs of Warrant

> "Over the course of the next few weeks No. 129 Squadron continued to bomb and 'strafe the Horrid Hun' to some effect, but losing three pilots, with only one surviving and captured"

Officer R. Thomas and Pilot Officer G. Pyle shot from the sky, both men surviving. Over the next few weeks No. 129 Squadron continued to bomb and "strafe the Horrid Hun" to some effect, but losing three pilots, with only one surviving and captured.

Success – but at a cost

No. 198 Squadron's diary similarly records considerable success in ground attacks. For example on 7 June, 'Pilots of "A" Flight rose early this morning and then took to the air at 0820 when S/Ldr I.J. Davies DFC, led 12 a/c on an Armed Recce to the Lisieux area. After crossing the French Coast our a/c proceeded to the appointed area and after patrolling the area for a short while 2 AFVs and a car were sighted N.W. of Cormeilles and attacked. Both AFVs were hit by RPs and left on fire. Later South of Bourg-Achard 3 AMC, 2 MeTs and a car were sighted and attacked. 2 of the AMCs and 1 Met were destroyed and the remainder were damaged; 2 Tanks were also attacked in the same area but no results were observed. It was during these attacks that Green 4 (W/O G.J. Stokes, Aus) was seen to have a small fire under his port wing. He pulled up to 1,500 ft, jettisoning

Above: Typhoon 1b JR197 'T' flown by Squadron Leader I. J. Davies DFC on 22 June 1944.
Below: Mustang III FZ121 'V' flown by Flight Lieutenant A. J. Hancock DFC and Bar on 22 June 1944.

PETE WEST

his hood as he did so, and then the a/c dived towards the earth and crashed in flames. It is possible that W/O Stokes managed to bale out, but no one reported having seen any sign of a parachute in the air and it is feared that W/O Stokes lost his life. A very unfortunate incident on an otherwise very successful operation.' W/O Stokes had indeed lost his life. In the following two weeks Squadron Leader Davies would lead his fellow pilots on further intense and successful ground-attack operations. But there was a cost, the squadron losing 7 Typhoons, with 5 of the respective pilots losing their lives.

One of the key elements to the success of the Normandy battle, once the beachhead was secured, was to break out to capture port facilities. On 16 June 1944 the Americans had attacked westward from Utah beach and within two days had forced their way through to the coastal village of Barneville, thereby cutting the Cotentin Peninsula. Within a day the American VIIth Corps swung north in order to assault Cherbourg, attempting to capture the vital port, so crucial to the Allied supply situation.

On 19 June Montebourg was overrun by the Americans, as was Valognes the following day. The Germans were pulling their forces back into a ring of defensive positions outside Cherbourg. To date the fighter-bombers of the American IXth Air Force had met the requirements of the push for Cherbourg. But when the Americans reached the fortified line around Cherbourg further air power was required to break the crust.

With a ground assault scheduled for 1400 hours on 22 June, the Allied airmen were tasked with bombing gun positions, strongpoints, troop concentrations and weapon dumps prior to the advance. On the day itself, two hours before the scheduled

**ALLAN JOHN HANCOCK
DFC AND BAR**

Rank: Flight Lieutenant (Pilot)
Unit: 129 Squadron
Date of Death: 22/06/1944
Service No: 120710
Age: 26
Son of John and Beatrice Asgil Hancock, of Houghton, Huntingdonshire.
Place of Burial: Bayeux War Cemetery – Grave/Memorial Reference: II. G. 7.

Inscribed on John Hancock's headstone, 'He rests in goodly company in a corner of a foreign field that is forever England'.

IDWAL JAMES DAVIES DFC

Rank: Squadron Leader (Pilot)
Unit: 198 Squadron
Date of Death: 22/06/1944
Service No: 63418
Age: 29
Son of Joseph and Maud Davies; husband of Irene Mary Davies, of Cheltenham, Gloucestershire.
Place of Burial: Bayeux War Cemetery – Grave/Memorial Reference: II. G. 3.

Inscribed on Idwal Davies's headstone, 'Our life together was short but sweet, God grant again that we shall meet'.

ground offensive the American troops withdrew 1,000 yards and their artillery unleashed an anti-flak barrage. First in came four rocket projectile Typhoon squadrons and six Mustang squadrons of the RAF's 2nd Tactical Air Force to attack strongpoints between 1240 and 1300 hours. In the wake of the RAF pilots came scores of Thunderbolts, the equivalent of 46 squadrons of American and RAF fighters wreaking havoc in just over 90 minutes. Flying in the initial attack were the pilots of No. 129 Squadron and No. 198 Squadron, encountering intense opposition from the ground.

'A disastrous day'

The No. 129 Squadron diarist opened his account of 22 June thus, 'A disastrous day'.

'Shortly after lunch the squadron [1207 hours], consisting of twelve aircraft, took off the strafe various selected targets in Cherbourg. Immediate misfortune occurred when F/Lt. A.L. Hancock, "B" Flight Commander, an extremely popular member of the squadron was shot down in flames by light flak. This unlucky break was instantly followed by F/Lt. A.C. Leigh, "A" Flight Commander receiving a direct hit in the sump, necessitating a hasty retreat from the immediate attentions of the Boche, in the area, and an ensuing forced landing on an American Emergency Landing Strip. The only bright thing about the whole show was that F/Lt. Leigh was uninjured and many Hun troops and vehicles injured.'

The No. 198 Squadron diary recorded, '11 a/c led by S/Ldr Davies DFC with 12 a/c of 609 Squadron went to Cherbourg [take-off 1205 hours] to give close support for the attack the Americans were launching in the afternoon. Strikes by R.P. and cannon were seen on flak positions,

STEVE DARLOW

Left: Two vintage images, viewed as a panorama. As the battle progressed in Normandy, a field was chosen near Bayeux in which to gather those who had lost their lives.

ERIC GUNTON/WILLIAM JORDAN BY PERMISSION

barrack blocks, railways and roads, and on a wireless station in the target area. The Squadron suffered another loss, this time our C.O., who was hit by flak and tried to make for our lines with a dead motor. At approximately a hundred feet over the American lines he baled out and his parachute did not fill out before he hit the ground. Although S/Ldr Davies had only been with us for just over a fortnight, he had proved himself a very able and popular C.O. and it is a very sad loss.'

Both Davies and Hancock had lost their lives.

Marauders had followed up the fighter-bomber attacks, at H-Hour, and the IXth Air Force continued the support of the ground offensive throughout the day. An official RAF history of the Normandy campaign records, 'Subsequent examination of gun positions hollowed out of rock appeared to show that no physical damage was done by bombing these well protected targets but accuracy on other targets was fair to good. There seemed to be no doubt that the morale effect of the air bombardment by low flying aircraft was overwhelming and this is confirmed by reliable evidence from the Germans' own reports. Lieutenant Colonel Hoffman of the Schlieben Group defending Cherbourg reporting on the situation to HQ German Seventh Army on the evening of the 24 June said that the troops "were worn down by the incessant

bombardment by enemy naval artillery and by air attacks." Strong points had clearly suffered heavy losses owing to air attacks.

Progress on the ground was initially slow, but relentless pressure and further air bombardments forced the Germans into Cherbourg's inner defences, which held out until 26 June, when most of the defenders submitted to the inevitable. By the end of the month all resistance had been snubbed out and work began to open up Cherbourg's port facilities.

Initially John Hancock and Idwal Davies were buried in St Mère Eglise US Military Cemetery. News of the award of a Bar to John Hancock's DFC was published after his death in action. Both their remains were transferred to Bayeux War Cemetery in February 1945. ■

When you go home
Tell them of us and say
For your tomorrow
We gave our today

The Normandy town of Bayeux is 24 kilometres north-west of Caen. The Bayeux Commonwealth War Cemetery can be found next to the town bypass (Rue de Sir Fabian Ware) to the south-west. The cemetery contains 4,144 Commonwealth World War Two burials, and 338 of these graves contain the remains of men yet to be identified. The cemetery also holds the remains of over 500 men of other nationalities, predominantly German. Opposite the cemetery is the Bayeux Memorial recording the names of 1,800 men of the Commonwealth land forces who have no known graves.

Thanks to: Chris Thomas, Chris Goss, Roy Hemington (CWGC Archive Supervisor), Mark Crame, William Jordan, and John Cripps.

Sources: Further details of John Hancock's career can be found in Chris Shores and Clive Williams's *Aces High*. Further details of Idwal Davies' career can be found in Chris Shores *Those Other Eagles*.

Night Fight over France

In support of Operation Overlord, the assault on the beaches of Normandy in June 1944 and the subsequent land battle, RAF Bomber Command carried out an intensive bombing campaign against the communication infrastructure of northern France and Belgium. This also included attacks on special targets such as secret weapon installations and German troop positions. The switch from bombing German targets to ones closer to home initially resulted in a decline in loss rates. However, on some operations the German night fighters did manage to penetrate the bomber streams and inflict serious losses. One such occasion was the raid to the German military camp at Mailly-le-Camp on the night of 3/4 May 1944. The bombing was very successful indeed but the raid takes its place in the history of Bomber Command as one of the most intensely fought night battles over France. In this article two 'K' reports, provided by men who fought in this battle, graphically illustrate the perils of night combat.

Bomber Command's 1 and 5 Groups despatched 346 Lancasters and 14 Mosquitoes on the raid, accompanied by 2 Pathfinder Mosquitoes. Over the target the attacking crews were to receive their bombing instructions from the 'Controller', or 'Master of Ceremonies' who would assess the conditions and the marking and advise the main force bombers to aim their explosives accordingly. However, not everything went to plan; there were delays in transmitting orders to the main force and many crews had to remain over the target, circling and waiting. The German nightfighters arrived and German airmen and RAF airmen fought for their lives; 42 Lancasters failed to return.

The first 'K' report, concerning a No. 550 Squadron Lancaster crew, mentions the problems over the target, and also demonstrates the confusion that could result as a seven-man crew, under attack, tried to save their damaged bomber.

AIRCRAFT ILLUSTRATIONS: PETE WEST

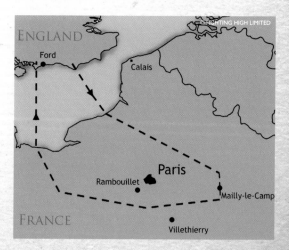

Top: Flight Sergeant Lloyd's 550 Squadron Lancaster.
Above: The bomber airmen's route to and from Mailly-le-Camp on the night of 3/4 May 1944.

REPORT ON LOSS OF AIRCRAFT ON OPERATIONS

AIRCRAFT	Lancaster III, ND733 'J' of 550 Squadron
DATE OF LOSS:	3/4 May 1944
TARGET:	Mailly-le-Camp
CAUSE OF LOSS:	Fighter attack, causing damage to controls and fire (Aircraft landed in England)
POSITION OF LOSS:	Near Dampierre (Rambouillet) homebound
INFORMATION FROM:	Sergeant Pearce, J.G., Mid Upper Gunner
REMAINDER OF CREW:	Captain & Pilot: Flight Sergeant Lloyd T. (Landed in England)
	Navigator: Warrant Officer Stephens D.M. (Landed in England)
	Wireless Operator: Sergeant Moore R.L.G. (Landed in England)
	Flight Engineer: Sergeant Burke T. (Landed in England)
	Air Bomber: Flying Officer Yatternick E. (Missing)
	Rear Gunner: Sergeant Crilley A. (Missing)

The Lancaster took off from Killingholme about 2200 hours. When the target area was reached, in bright moonlight, it was already illuminated by yellow and white flares round which the pilot circled as ordered at briefing. After circling the flares for a long time - about a quarter of an hour - the Master of Ceremonies gave the order "You may bomb now". They accordingly bombed the main target from a height of 5/6,000 ft., and set course on the homeward route.

At a point SW of Paris some heavy flak was encountered and, soon after, while informant was still standing up in his turret watching for flak, they were suddenly attacked by a fighter from underneath. The enemy was completely hidden from informant's position and must have been dead astern and below. Cannon fire struck the Lancaster "with terrific punch", smashing a hole in starboard tail-plane and starboard wing. Informant's turret was slightly damaged.

The Captain called up informant, who reported he was all right. He then called the Rear Gunner three times without receiving an answer. The Wireless Operator went aft to investigate but before he reached the rear turret the gunner called on the intercomm. that he had been slightly cut in the face. The Wireless Operator went to attend to him. Informant reported to the Captain such damage as he could see to the wings, and the latter announced he would make for Base, but would give immediate warning if he found that impossible. The aircraft was shuddering considerably, but the engineer stated the motors and petrol were all right.

The Navigator had just warned the Captain that they were heading straight for Paris, when he was interrupted by another terrific crash. Informant swung his turret and caught sight of the enemy as he broke away under the starboard wing. Informant opened fire with a very short burst, but claims no hits. At the same moment he heard the Captain call on the intercomm. "Abandon aircraft by parachute". (He did not say "prepare to abandon aircraft"). Informant now had difficulty in turning his turret, and all he could manage was to turn it half-way manually. Then he called up the Captain for confirmation of the order, but does not think he heard. Informant then called that he was going to bale out and wished the Captain good luck.

Before he got out of the mid-upper turret, informant saw the Wireless Operator running forward and then return aft, presumably with his parachute. When he entered the fuselage, informant found there was a fire in the bomb-bay, and in the fuselage above it. It was very hot, and there was much smoke. Oily flames could be seen through the open bomb-bay inspection panels as if fed by hydraulic fluid. Informant concluded that there must be something amiss in the front of the aircraft as no one was ordered to use the extinguishers, and he considered that the Captain might not be able to see the fire.

Informant had planned to bale out from the rear exit and, after fetching his parachute from the starboard side of the fuselage - he had to pass through the flames to get it - he made his way aft. At the rear door there was a lot of wreckage, possibly part of the H2S equipment, which he dragged away to clear the exit. The Rear Gunner and Wireless Operator were crouching against the port side of the fuselage, and informant opened the door and motioned them to go, but they did not move. The aircraft was fairly stable, but nothing more was heard from the Captain. Informant sat on the step at the door, with his feet out, and states that he was given a strong push from behind, possibly by the Wireless Operator, and he fell clear of the aircraft.

His parachute opened satisfactorily, but the harness cut his face and forced his head down so that he did not see what happened to the aircraft. There was no sign of it when he eventually managed to free his head and he thought it might have flown on towards Base. He landed successfully in a ditch with his 'chute in telegraph wires, about 2 kilometres from Dampierre, Rambouillet, SW of Paris.

ORS COMMENT

The Lancaster crash-landed at Ford, at 0255 hours on 4 May, and damage was classed as Cat. El, slightly burnt. The Captain and Wireless Operator were uninjured but suffered from shock, the latter only mildly. The Navigator and Flight Engineer received superficial burns, the former also suffering from shock.

These members of the crew reported as follows.

After attacking the target the Lancaster was hit by a flak burst around the tail and port wing. VISUAL MONICA was rendered unserviceable and the Rear Gunner, whose face had been injured, left his turret on the Captain's orders. The Mid Upper Gunner continued the search, remaining in his own turret. About 5 minutes after the flak damage, i.e. 0109 hours (at 4819N 0215E, height 12,000 ft.) the crew felt and saw tracer bullets coming at them from the port quarter down, but no attacking aircraft was seen. (Moon on the port beam, clear visibility). Immediately the bomber burst into flames and dived down out of control. The Captain ordered the crew to bale out. The Rear Gunner, Mid Upper Gunner, and Bomb Aimer carried out these orders, but before the rest got out the Captain "realised the position and struggled with the controls, which by now responded and control of the aircraft was maintained". The fire was got under control, and the Lancaster made England.

This statement confirms the main points in informant's narrative. Inspection of the damaged aircraft confirms the latter's statement that all the enemy action was caused by fighter, not by flak. The holes reported by informant in main and tail-plane were on the port, not starboard side. The aileron and elevator controls were also found to be damaged, as well as the rear turret.

20 JULY 1944

Flight Sergeant Lloyd had managed to regain control of the Lancaster by wrapping his arms and legs around the control column, with the aid of his flight engineer, Sergeant Burke, who occasionally took the load. In the meantime, using extinguishers, hands, feet, and coffee flasks, Sergeant Burke and Sergeant Moore managed to quell the flames. When they approached Ford, Lloyd would later recall that the runway lights looked like 'a glimpse of heaven' and he belly-landed the Lancaster, which would be written off. Lloyd, Sergeant Moore and Sergeant Burke each received the Distinguished Flying Medal. Flying Officer Yatternick and Sergeant Crilley had

survived the incident and it is believed they also managed to evade capture.

The second 'K' report shows how luck played its part when it came to surviving a combat with a nightfighter. Also note that this crew had some 'thirds' of operations to their credit. RAF Bomber Command had adopted a policy of not counting operations to targets in certain areas in the German-occupied territories as whole operations with regard to working towards a full tour of, usually for main force, 30 raids. Raids such as that to Mailly-le-Camp caused many crews to question such a policy.

REPORT ON LOSS OF AIRCRAFT ON OPERATIONS

AIRCRAFT   Lancaster I, ME697 'A' of 625 Squadron
DATE OF LOSS   3/4 May 1944
TARGET   Mailly-le-Camp
CAUSE OF LOSS   Fire caused by fighter attack, homebound
POSITION OF LOSS Villethierry (Yonne), 10 miles NW of Sens
INFORMATION FROM Sergeant Evans, P.J. Wireless Operator, on 13th (+ 1/3) operation
REMAINDER OF CREW Captain & Pilot: Squadron Leader Gray R.W.H., on 14th (+ 2/3) operation
                      Navigator: Flying Officer Medway L.F., on 16th (+ 2/3) operation
                      Flight Engineer: Flying Officer Martin D.C., on 8th (+ 1/3) operation of 2nd tour
                      Air Bomber: Flight Sergeant Footman W.A., on 14th (+ 1/3) operation
                      Mid-Upper-Gunner: Pilot Officer Johnson J.G., on 20th operation
                      Rear Gunner: Sergeant Escritt B., on 19th operation

Above: Flight Sergeant Walter Footman who flew as the air bomber of the No. 625 Squadron Lancaster.

The Lancaster took off from Kelstern at 2152 hours. Before leaving England GEE became unserviceable, and H2S became unserviceable at the French coast.

The target area was reached earlier than intended, but the target was already well alight. Lancaster 'A' was one of the 30 aircraft detailed to attack a concentration of tanks, and bombed the aiming point from 6,000 ft. in bright moonlight.

Not long after setting course on the homeward route, which lay south of Paris, height then being about 8,000 ft., informant heard the Rear Gunner report that the rear part of the Lancaster was on fire. Informant had previously been listening in to broadcasts, and this was the first intimation he had of the attack. FISHPOND was not working because of the H2S failure. He gathered that the fire had been caused by a fighter, but that none of the crew, with the possible exception of the Rear Gunner, had seen it. The Lancaster had been flying straight and level before the attack after which the Rear Gunner warned the Captain to "keep diving to port".

As soon as he heard the report of the fire, informant seized the extinguisher and went aft towards the fire. As he did so, the Mid Upper Gunner passed him going forward with his parachute. The Gunner said nothing, but informant concluded that the Captain had ordered the crew to prepare to abandon the aircraft. He, therefore, plugged in to the intercomm., heard the Rear Gunner say the flames were reaching his arm, and then went forward with his parachute. He found the Air Bomber, Navigator and Mid Upper Gunner standing by the escape hatch in the nose, and the Flight Engineer was clipping on the Pilot's parachute. Informant opened the window on the starboard side of the Pilot's cockpit to disperse the smoke from the fire. In the fuselage the fire was now too large to control, although informant used his extinguisher as far back as his own compartment and eventually left it pointing towards the blaze. He returned and stood beside the Captain waiting for the order to jump. He had already checked that the 4,000 lb bomb had released at the target, and saw that there was no fire in the wing.

The next thing informant recalls is floating down on his parachute. He is certain he did not leave the aircraft by the escape hatch and he does not remember pulling his ripcord. He believes that he may have been thrown out of the aircraft from a height of about 4/5,000 ft. On landing he found he had sprained his back and ankle. Position was at the village of Villethierry, 10 miles NW of Sens and about 50 miles SE of Paris. The time was roughly 0200 hours.

After landing, informant saw a Lancaster being followed by a fighter. He was told later that five members of his crew were buried at St. Agnain cemetery. Two were said to have been found burned in the wreckage of the aircraft, three others nearby with parachutes - perhaps thrown out like informant. An airman called "Gray", possibly the Captain, was said to be safe.

Sergeant Gray had indeed survived, and was captured.

WHERE THE AIRMEN LIE

The five men who lost their lives in the incident involving the No. 625 Squadron Lancaster – Leslie Medway (aged 20), David Martin (aged 28), Walter Footman (aged 24), John Johnson (aged 31), and Benjamin Escritt (aged 23) – are buried at St Agnan communal cemetery (note the misspelling in the 'K' report). St Agnan village is a few kilometres north-west of Villethierry, 30 kilometres east-south-east of Fontainebleau, and 20 kilometres north-west of Sens, France. The cemetery is on the north side of the village on a minor road leading north (direction of Villeneuve-la-Guyard) from the church.

Right: St Agnan Cemetery and the memorial to the crew.

Right: A detail of the memorial St Agnan Cemetery.

YVONNE KINSELLA

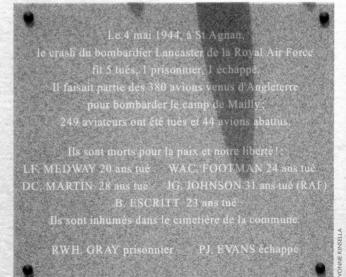

Le 4 mai 1944, à St Agnan,
le crash du bombardier Lancaster de la Royal Air Force
fit 5 tués, 1 prisonnier, 1 échappé.
Il faisait partie des 380 avions venus d'Angleterre
pour bombarder le camp de Mailly.
249 aviateurs ont été tués et 44 avions abattus.

Ils sont morts pour la paix et notre liberté !
LF. MEDWAY 20 ans tué   WAC. FOOTMAN 24 ans tué
DC. MARTIN 28 ans tué   JG. JOHNSON 31 ans tué (RAF)
B. ESCRITT 23 ans tué
Ils sont inhumés dans le cimetière de la commune.

RWH. GRAY prisonnier   PJ. EVANS échappé

YVONNE KINSELLA

LESLIE MEDWAY
Rank: Flying Officer (Pilot)
Regiment/Service:
Royal Air Force Volunteer Reserve
Unit: No. 625 Squadron
Age: 20
Date of Death: 04/05/1944
Service No: 143849
Son of Frank Stanley and Caroline Alice Medway, of Sawbridgeworth, Hertfordshire.
Place of Burial: St Agnan Communal Cemetery, Plot E, Row 1, Joint grave 4–5.

DAVID MARTIN
Rank: Flying Officer (Flt Engr.)
Regiment/Service: Royal Air Force
Unit: No. 625 Squadron
Age: 28
Date of Death: 04/05/1944
Service No: 52312
Son of Charles Martin, DCM, and Catherine Martin; husband of Anne Martin, of Battersea, London.
Place of Burial: St Agnan Communal Cemetery, Plot E, Row 1, Grave 3.

WALTER FOOTMAN
Rank: Flight Sergeant (Air Bomber)
Regiment/Service:
Royal Air Force Volunteer Reserve
Unit: No. 625 Squadron
Age: 24
Date of Death: 04/05/1944
Service No: 1391733
Son of Walter Ernest and Ella Footman, husband of Phyllis Irene Footman, of Bournville, Birmingham.
Place of Burial: St Agnan Communal Cemetery, Plot E, Row 1, Joint grave 4–5.

JOHN JOHNSON
Rank: Pilot Officer (Air Gnr.)
Regiment/Service: Royal Canadian Air Force
Unit: No. 625 Squadron
Age: 31
Date of Death: 04/05/1944
Service No: J/85585
Son of John William and Susan Johnson.
Place of Burial: St Agnan Communal Cemetery, Plot E, Row 1, Grave 1.

BENJAMIN ESCRITT
Rank: Sergeant (Air Gnr.)
Regiment/Service:
Royal Air Force Volunteer Reserve
Unit: No. 625 Squadron
Age: 23
Date of Death: 04/05/1944
Service No: 1071465
Son of Benjamin and Edith Clara Escritt, of Hull.
Place of Burial: St Agnan Communal Cemetery, Plot E, Row 1, Grave 2.

Left: Despite the losses on the Mailly-le-Camp raid, the Bomber Command attack caused widespread destruction – as evidenced by these before and after photographs. Martin Middlebrook and Chris Everitt record in *The Bomber Command War Diaries* that 114 barrack buildings, 47 transport sheds and some ammunition buildings were hit; 102 vehicles, of which 37 were tanks, were destroyed, 218 German soldiers were killed, and 156 were injured.

ℹ Further accounts from those involved in the Mailly-le-Camp raid can be found in Steve Darlow's book *Special Op: Bomber*.

Sources. 'K' reports held at the National Archives, Commonwealth War Graves Commission website www.cwgc.org, ww2images.com website. Thanks to Jack Harris OBE, DFC and Yvonne Kinsella for the use of her photographs.

Life as a Kriegie, incarcerated in a Stalag Luft, was tough, mentally and physically. Days and nights, more days and nights, and even more days and nights behind wire could drive men mad. Various efforts were made to occupy the thoughts of the fallen Allied airmen: gardening, studying, sport, books, drama, and some enjoyed recording their experiences and thoughts with personal illustrations. The logbooks of the POWs often contain details of such scribblings and here is a selection of 'doodles' from the log of RAF Bomber Command pilot **Arthur Darlow**.

Kriegie Doodles

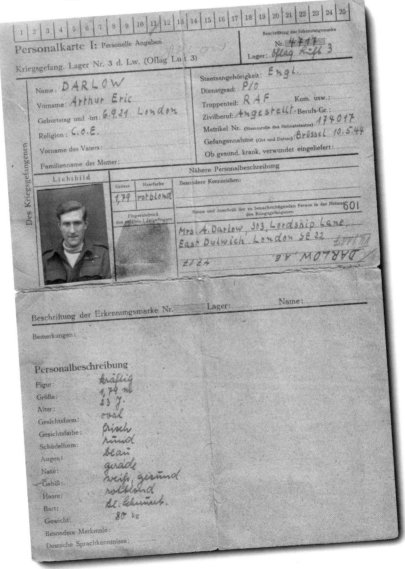

Right: Arthur's POW identity card.

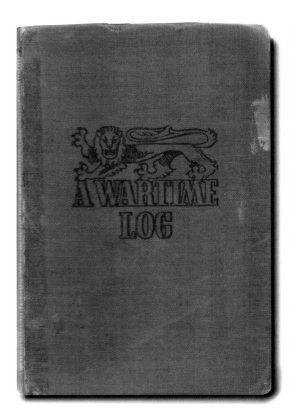

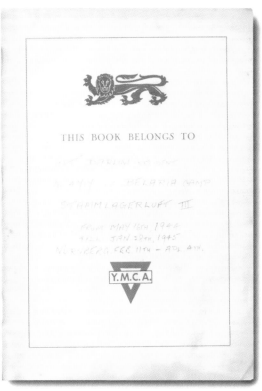

Left: Front cover and title page of Arthur's POW logbook.

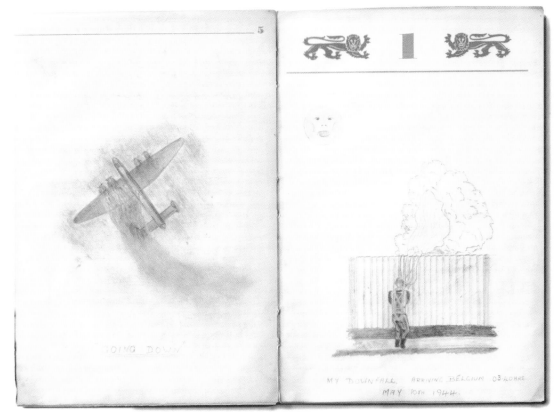

Arthur Darlow, then flying as a Pathfinder pilot with No. 405 Squadron (RCAF), was shot down in May 1944 on the return flight from a raid to Haine St. Pierre.

Arthur held his burning aircraft whilst five of his crew made a sharp exit. Three men would go on to evade capture. Arthur and two others would not be so fortunate, although they did survive. The rear gunner lost his life, believed killed in the aircraft.

Arthur was captured the morning after being shot down, ending up at Stalag Luft III's Belaria compound a few weeks later, where he sketched his downfall.

Right: The layout of Arthur's new home village. He was housed in room 7, block 6.

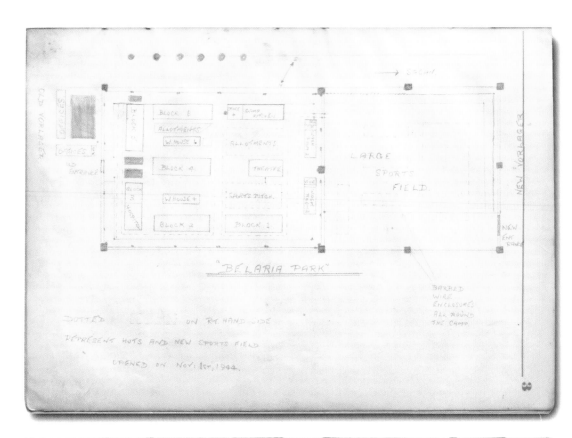

Right: With time on his hands a Kriegie's mind wanders to what the future may hold.

Left: The sleeping arrangements at 'Hotel Belaria' as Arthur described it. Spartan to say the least, but perhaps the views from the windows made up for it...

...Perhaps not!

Right: Just before Arthur reached Stalag Luft III, the mass break-out, immortalised as the 'Great Escape', led to the execution of 50 of the escapees. Here, beneath some striking imagery, Arthur lists most of the 50.

Left: It is unclear if spinach was actually on the Kriegie menu.

Below: A night out (well not literally).

Left: The language of Kriegie life.

''Belaria''

Here we sit in Stalag
Luft III
Drinking in the bar.
With lovely girls to buy
the rounds.
Like bloody hell! we are.

We travelled here in
luxury.
The whole trip for a
quid.
A sleeping berth for
each of us.
Like bloody hell! we did.

Our feather beds are
two feet deep.
The carpets almost new.
In easy chairs we sit all
day.
Like bloody hell! we do.

The goons are darned
wizard chaps.
Their hopes of Victory
good.
We'd change their
places any day.
Like bloody hell! we
would.

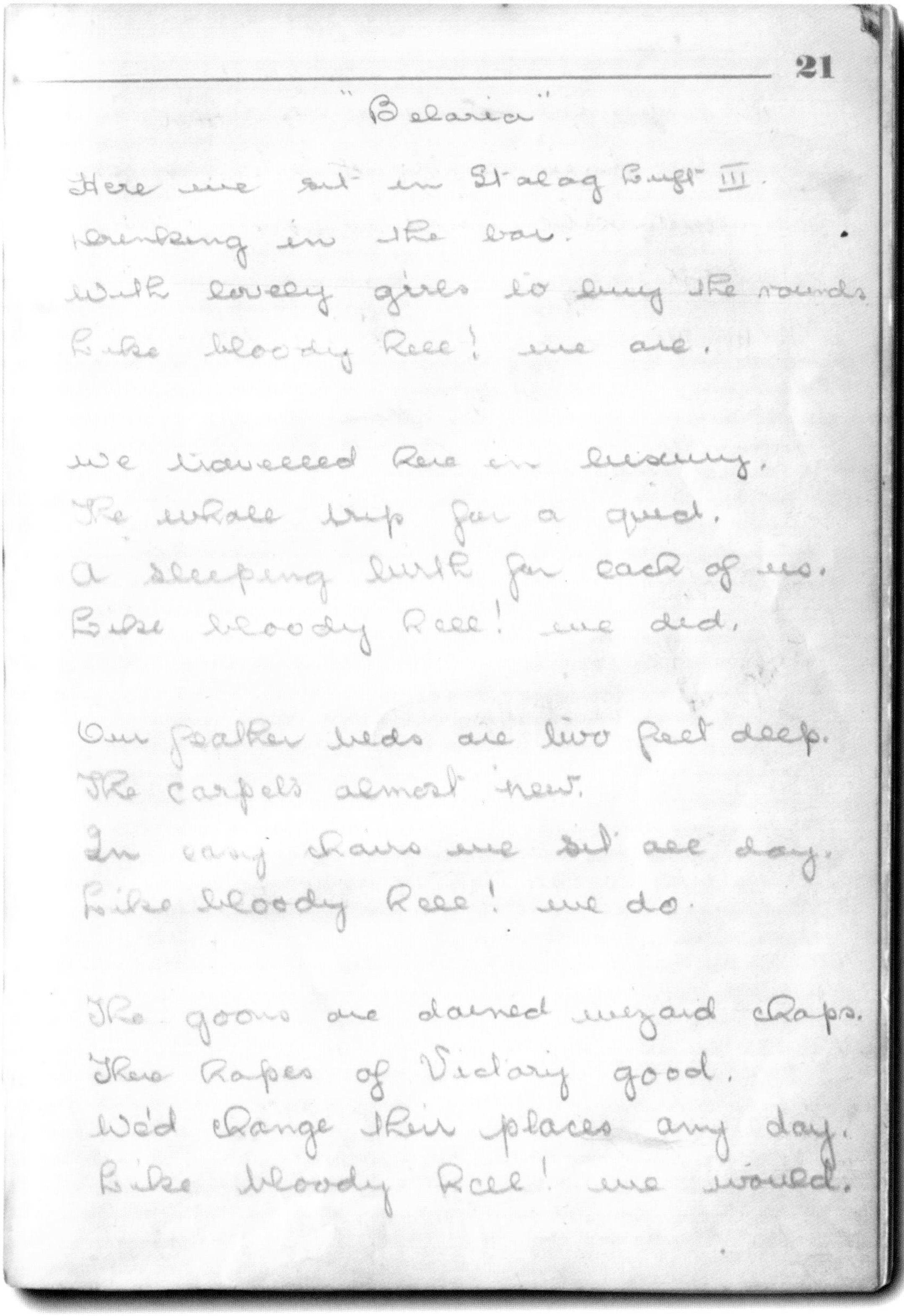

21

"Belaria"

Here we sit in Stalag Luft III.
Drinking in the bar.
With lovely girls to buy the rounds
Like bloody hell! we are.

We travelled here in luxury.
The whole trip for a quid.
A sleeping berth for each of us.
Like bloody hell! we did.

Our feather beds are two feet deep.
The carpets almost new.
In easy chairs we sit all day.
Like bloody hell! we do.

The goons are darned wizard chaps.
Their hopes of Victory good.
We'd change their places any day.
Like bloody hell! we would.

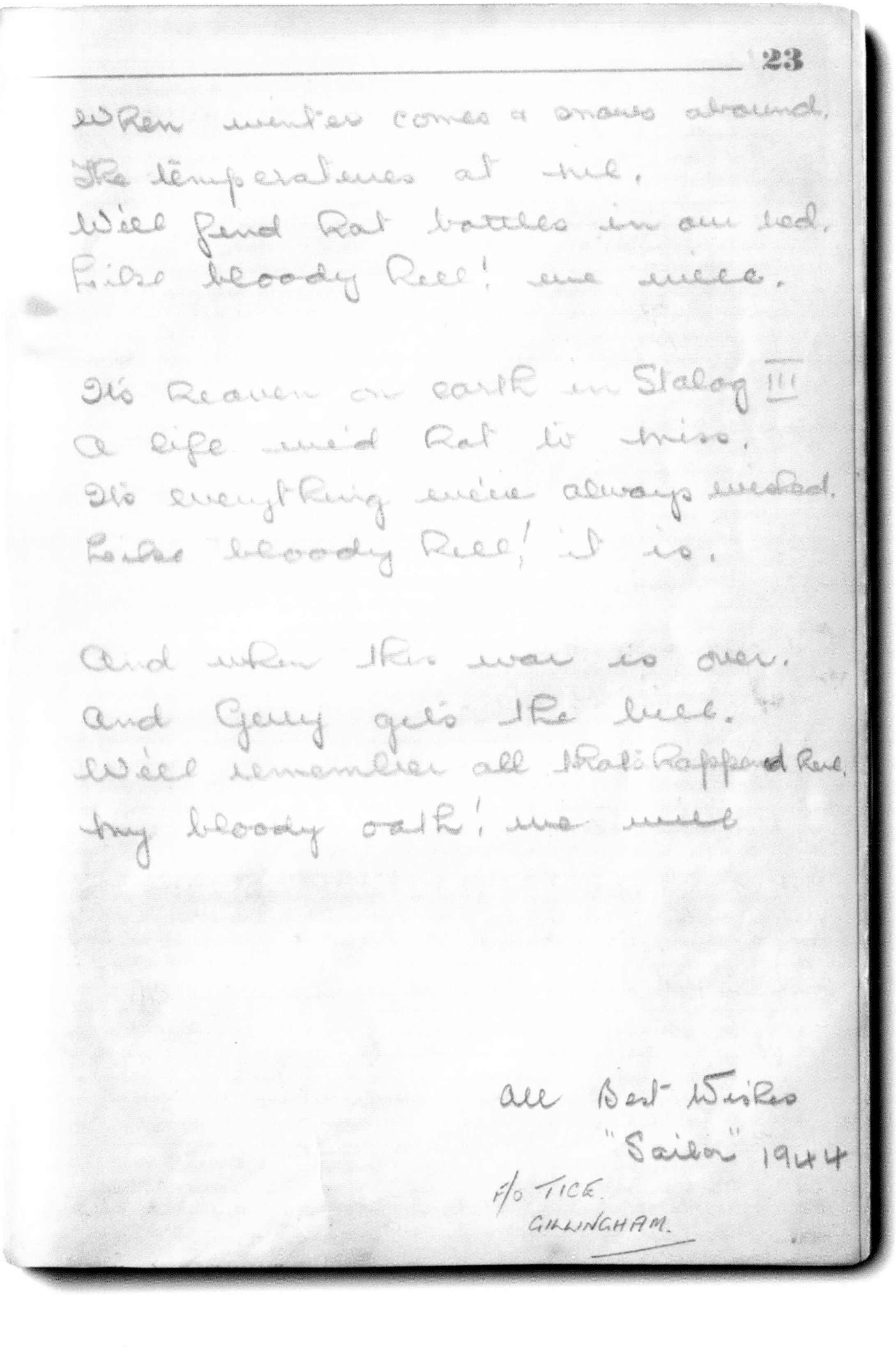

When winter comes & snows abound,
The temperatures at nil,
We'll find Rat battles in our Sod,
Like bloody Hell! we will.

Its Heaven on earth in Stalag III
A life we'd Rat to miss,
Its everything we've always wished,
Like bloody Hell! it is.

And when this war is over.
And Gerry gets the bill.
We'll remember all that's Rapped Rec.
My bloody oath! we will

All Best Wishes
"Sailor" 1944
F/o Tice.
Gillingham.

When winter comes & snows abound
The temperatures at nil.
We'll find hot bottles in our bed.
Like bloody hell! we will.

Its heaven on earth in Stalag III
A life we'd hate to miss.
Its everything we've always wished.
Like bloody hell! it is.

And when the war is over.
And Gerry gets the bill.
We'll remember all that's happened here.
My bloody oath! we will.

All Best Wishes
"Sailor" 1944

F/O Tice
Gillingham

CHAPTER SIXTEEN

Ace
Mosquito Team

Left: The outstanding Mosquito pairing of Russ Bannock (left) and his navigator 'Bob' Bruce.

Wing Commander Russell Bannock's citations for the various gallantry awards won serving with the Royal Canadian Air Force in the United Kingdom during World War Two, highlight his extreme skill and courage: 'a highly efficient flight commander'; 'much skill and initiative' (Distinguished Flying Cross); 'outstanding ability, great determination and devotion to duty'; 'sterling qualities' (Bar to DFC); 'As squadron commander, Wing Commander Bannock has proved to be an outstanding success' (Distinguished Service Order).

At the end of the war Bannock, with his navigator 'Bob' Bruce, whilst flying with No. 418 and No. 406 Squadrons, had accounted for 9 enemy aircraft destroyed, 4 damaged, 2 destroyed on the ground, and 18 and 1 shared V-1s, placing them as one of the most outstanding Mosquito pairings of the war.

AIRCRAFT ILLUSTRATION: PETE WEST

INTELLIGENCE FORM 'F' AND PILOTS PERSONAL COMBAT REPORT
418 SQUADRON - RAF HOLMSLEY SOUTH

Date...June 14/15 1944
Unit, Flight, Squadron........................418 (RCAF) City of Edmonton Squadron
Type and mark of our aircraft ....One Mosquito VI
Time attack was delivered..0143 hours
Place of attack...Avord Airfield
Weather.....................................Very dark, some high cloud
Our Casualties - aircraft..Nil
Our casualties - personnel ....Nil
Enemy Casualties in air combat.........................1 Me110 destroyed
Enemy Casualties - ground or sea targets.........................Nil

General
One Mosquito VI S/L Bannock (Pilot), F/O Bruce (Observer), took off from Holmsley
South at 2301 on Flower operation to Bourges and Avord Airfields, landed back at base
0328 hours.

"In at Avranches at 2347 and arrived in target area at 0055. Avord A/F lit
with E/W V/L eastern arm only with two crossbars, double white flarepath, and red
perimeter lights. Steady white beacon 8 miles S.E. of Avord. We concentrated our
patrol along downwind leg of Avord A/F. At 0125 double red fired from Avord, and all
lights doused, and 4 searchlights came on which failed to engage. We left to visit
Bourges and Chateauroux. We returned again at 0130, V/L on again, but on approach
another double red fired and lights doused but only for a minute, then on again. We
continued patrol of downwind leg and at 0142 saw D.R.L flashing ahead and above and

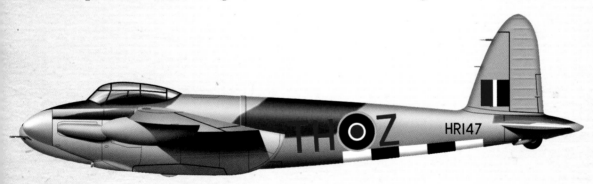

obtained a visual momentarily of an aircraft flying east in opposite direction to us.
We turned sharply to starboard but lost visual. We flew directly towards the outer
bar of V/L where a vertical S/L was flicked on. At the same time we saw aircraft over
inner bar again flashing D.R.L. We gave chase closed to 500 yards, firing a 1 second
burst at 40° angle off to port. At the same time, airfield defences opened up with
intense accurate light flak from eastern end of A/F. We broke to port, noticing
aircraft turn on landing light, just after he touched down. We made a hard starboard
turn attacking E/A at approximately 90° on position of the way down runway from 400
feet opening fire with 2 second burst from 400 yards. Strikes seen on centre section
of fuselage and wingroot, E/A almost immediately catching fire. In the light of the
explosion we identified E/A as Me110. At this stage we were engaged by flak and
searchlights came up. We broke to port, noticing E/A burning fiercely on the runway.
Two more searchlights coned us but we managed to break away and set course for base.
V/L was still on when we left and burning aircraft seen from some distance away.

INTELLIGENCE FORM 'F' AND PILOTS PERSONAL COMBAT REPORT
418 SQUADRON - RAF HUNSDON

Date ....27 September 1944
Unit, Flight, Squadron...............................418 (RCAF) City of Edmonton Squadron
Type and mark of our aircraft ....1 Mosquito VI
Time attack was delivered ....06:15 & 06:16 hours
Place of attack ....Parrow A.F
Weather ....C.A.V.U.
Our Casualties - aircraft ....1 Mosquito VI, Cat. A.
Our casualties - personnel ....Nil
Enemy Casualties in air combat 2 Me108s
Enemy Casualties - ground or sea targets...Nil

General
One Mosquito VI, S/L Bannock (Pilot), F/O Bruce (Observer), took off from Hunsdon at 0352
hours, on a Day Ranger to Bug/Aufrugun, landed base 1015 hours. Crossed in over enemy coast at
Egmond at 0437 hours.

"We flew across N. Germany at about 200 ft, and as dawn broke we gradually went down to
tree top level. Crossed the Elbe S.E. of Bremen and there flew directly to Kubetizer Bay, via
Muritz Lake. As we were about 2 miles West of Parrow A/F we noticed six S.E. training aircraft
that had just taken off. We attempted to get on the tail of a Bucker 131 but he saw us making our
approach and easily out-manoeuvred us. We then attacked an Me108 with his wheels down in the
downwind leg of the circuit at 1,000 ft. We fired a 1-second burst from dead astern at 200 yards
and the E/A blew up, crashing into Kubetizer Bay at 0615 hours. We attacked a second Me108 at
0616 hours in approximately the same position, making a 90° beam attack, firing a 1-burst with
two rings deflection. The E/A caught fire in the cockpit area, rolled over onto its back and
dived into the sea. At this point F/O Bruce said that an E/A was attacking us from the port
quarter. I immediately turned port into the attack and was going to open fire in a head on
attack when I noticed that this aircraft was trying to ram us. I broke away to starboard, diving
below the aircraft. This E/A which was also an Me108 did a sharp turn on to our tail and opened
fire from about 500 yards. Bullets were seen hitting the water below us. We easily pulled away
from the E/A and flew north of the A/F. We noticed the temp. on the port engine had risen to 120,
almost immediately the port engine caught fire. I feathered the port engine and used the fire
extinguisher. As soon as the flames had gone out we set course for base, flying across the
Baltic and Denmark at tree top height. We crossed out over the enemy coast just north of Sylt.
Crossed back in over the English coast in the vicinity of Felixstowe.

Upon arrival at base we discovered that a piece of Perspex from the first E/A dest. had
penetrated our port engine rad. which had resulted in a glycol leak and the subsequent fire.
Cine Camera Gun automatically exposed."

Ammunition used: Browning, P.O. 28, P.I. 28, S.I. 27, S.O. 29
                      Cannon, P.O. 32, P.I. 33, S.I. 32, S.O. 35

INTELLIGENCE FORM 'F' AND PILOTS PERSONAL COMBAT REPORT
418 SQUADRON - RAF HUNSDON

Date ....30 September 1944
Unit, Flight, Squadron ....418 (RCAF) City of Edmonton Squadron
Type and mark of our aircraft .... 2 Mosquitoes VI
Time attack was delivered .... 1045 hours
Place of attack .... Vaerloese A/F
Weather .... Clear 1/10ths cloud 5,000 feet
Our Casualties - aircraft ....1 Mosquito VI (S/L Bannock) Cat. AC due flak
Our casualties - personnel ....Nil
Enemy Casualties in air combat ....Nil
Enemy Casualties - ground or sea targets ......1 Ju88, 1 Me110 destroyed in ground by S/L Bannock
1 FW190, 1 Me110 damaged in ground by F/O Seid

General Report

Two Mosquitoes VI, S/L Bannock (Pilot) F/O Bruce (Observer) and F/O Seid (Pilot) F/O McIntosh (Observer) took off from Coltishall at 0824 hours on a Day Ranger to the Copenhagen area and landed at Hunsdon 1340 hours.

S/L Bannock states:

"We crossed the North German coast at Pellworm 0944 hours and flew East across north Germany into the Baltic as far as Rodby. Whilst in the Baltic we experienced light and heavy flak from a ship 4 miles S. of Downs Cliff.

We approached Vaerloese A/F at zero feet from the south west and saw 3 FW190s parked in front of a hangar and what appeared to be the Control Tower. Because of the hangar we were poorly positioned for an attack. We then circled the A/F to the east where we observed a Ju88 which was parked at the eastern extremity of the A/F. We then turned hard to port and opened fire on this a/c with 1-secs burst of cannon and machine gun from approximately 100 yards. Numerous strikes were seen on the port wing root and cockpit area. A sheet of flames immediately shot out of port petrol tank enveloping the cockpit area. Shortly after passing over this aircraft I did a hard turn to starboard and in doing so observed a column of black smoke pouting out of this aircraft.

Just after turning I observed another aircraft which was an Me110 parked in a blast bay on the north side of the A/F. I again attacked from 100 to 75 yards with a 1-secs burst of cannon and machine gun aiming for the wing root. A sheet of flame shot out of what must have been the port petrol tank. I then had to pull hard back on the control column to clear the blast bay and then flew north at tree top level as the flak had become particularly intense during the latter attack.

NB. An 'Erk' was working around the tail section of the Me110 as we approached and, after one look at us, he broke all speed records during a sprint in an easterly direction."

Left: Flight Lieutenant Russ Bannock (left) and navigator Flying Officer 'Bob' Bruce.

F/O Seid states:

"I followed S/L Bannock in from the east but as I was uncertain whether we intended attacking the A/F I was poorly positioned. Whilst still in a steep turn I noticed dense black smoke issuing for the Ju88 previously mentioned. I continued the turn and noticed several aircraft parked on the south side of the a/f and opened fire with 2 x 2 secs bursts of cannon. I was unable to concentrate fire on any particular object so endeavoured to strafe the line of three aircraft. Strikes were seen in front, through and beyond an Me110 and an FW190, but the extent of the damage could not be observed.

I commenced to position myself for a further attack, but S/L Bannock called up on R.T. and stated that it might not be "too healthy" to make another attack.

Since I concentrated my attack on the south of the a/f I did not see S/L Bannock make his second attack.

NB. During my attack another 'Erk' was observed descending a high ladder near the roof of a hangar. Upon seeing us the speed of his descent was suddenly and forcibly increased by a backward fall from near the top of the ladder. I claim this 'Erk' as probably destroyed." Cine Camera automatically exposed.

Armament Report:

S/L Bannock	Browning, P.O. 25, P.I. 24, S.I. 26, S.O. 27
	Cannon, P.O. 25, P.I. 25, S.I. 26, S.O. 28
F/O Seid	Cannon, P.O. 49 P.I. 48, S.I. 52, S.O. 48

DEAR MOM
JACK STYLES

Jack Styles had managed to navigate his heavily damaged bomber back from Germany, but now his skipper, Joe Talocka, was fighting hard to control their No. 426 Squadron Halifax VII, and land safely. They were returning from an attack on the Wanne-Eickel oil refinery, during which Halifax VII NP819 OW-B had been hit by flak, ripping up the starboard aileron and puncturing holes in the wings and the fuselage. With the ordeal nearly over Talocka twice had to pull out of a landing, as the RAF Manston runway was not lit. Those on the ground tried desperately to make contact with the crew. It is then thought that the aircraft hit a slip stream and went into a steep bank. The controls locked and the Halifax plunged to the ground from about 500 feet. The wireless operator managed to bale out in time. The rest of the crew did not.

Right:
Commonwealth War Graves Brookwood Military Cemetery.

STEVE DARLOW

Jack Styles was born in Midland, Ontario, Canada, in 1925, joining the Royal Canadian Air Force in 1943. Throughout his training and operational flying Jack kept in regular contact with his mother. A letter from Jack, addressed from London, Ontario, in October 1943 records the excitement of Jack's first flight.

Dear Mom

Boy was it wonderful. We got all dolled up in our flying clothes (I wish you could see me) which are much too big …The crotch of mine is half way to my knees. When we put our parachute on it pulled all the slack up making a big bulge to front and rear where there shouldn't be a bulge. We then went to briefing where we get our orders…to sit in the plane and watch the passing scenery and if we got sick we were to use the paper bags supplied and instead of bombing some poor unsuspecting church goers with them, to bring them back and place them in the nearest garbage can. We then went to our plane and took our seats. Since there was one more man than seats…I sat on the floor. The pilot then tried to get in touch with the control tower by radio but the damned radio wouldn't work. Fine!! Then he tried the motors and one wasn't working well. Swell!! We then all piled out of the plane and into another one (again I sat on the bloody floor)…we went to the edge of the runway and started down it. I was sitting there wondering when

we would reach the end of it when I happened to look out of the window. There was the ground only it was about 1000 feet below us. Wow!!

We started to fly along about 3000 feet and I started to enjoy myself. You look out and you see a little mist pass you. That was a cloud. You look down and you see a lot of little squares (the ground) with little lines (roads) and blue curved lines (rivers). Then you look at your map which has roads, rivers etc. on it and you try to find out where you are. Not finding it you decide you must have brought the wrong map. However on checking with the lucky so-and-so's in the seats you find that you have the right map but are looking at the wrong corner of it (you are never near the centre, that would be too easy). You look out again and you see what looks like a thin wood (that's a town) and so on …Then you put your map down and start to watch the scenery (against orders). The plane hits a pocket and your stomach feels funny after falling through the air. You decide you had better work than sit there thinking of those paper bags and what they are for. So you pick up your map and look out the window to try to find where you are. This being hopeless you ask the pilot. On locating yourself you find that there is supposed to be a racetrack somewhere under you but you can't see it through the wing so you tell the pilot. He gives the

wheel a turn (stick to you) and tells you to look out again. You look out and the wing is gone but the racetrack is there. Thinking that you have lost a wing you look around for the one on the other side. It is there standing straight up in the air, then you decide that you are on your side. You hastily tell the pilot that you have seen the racetrack and everything goes back on even keel. Right then and there you decide never again to ask him to let you see something …Fine, you decide you have a strong stomach by now so you commence to look around you…after about an hour you see something and venture to ask if that is London airport. Hurra you are right this time (now a veteran, never wrong) …the wing is gone again and that damn place starts to come right up toward you. That feels nice on your stomach …then the wing comes back up and the ground comes up faster until it is right under you. Bump you are down …[you see] the Interrogating officer who asks you who was sick. He seemed awfully sad when we said no one was. Then we went to dinner with our chests out and our heads held high. We were now veterans. We had flown. Boy oh boy. I am not kidding, it is swell…

This may not tell you much but it will give you an idea of my first flight in a flying boxcar, an Avro Anson.

Your loving son

(who didn't get sick) Jack

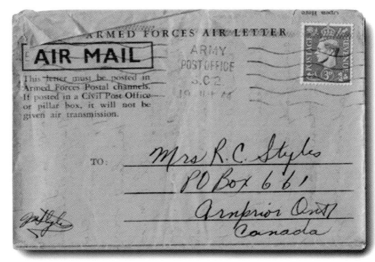

It is clear from Jack's letters that he had a close relationship with his mum, catching up on her welfare, sending money and flowers, 17 January 1944: 'Sure you are lonesome, so are about a million others. Chin up and I'll be home before you know it.' In the early months of Jack's training, there was not much to report. In fact, boredom was the enemy.

March 1944 No. 1 AGTS, Maitland, NS: *God what a hole. There is nothing to do here except sleep whenever you have spare time. Brother…I am going to increase my assignment to $90 per month soon. Do you think you can manage on that? Please write me. I have had no word from anybody yet & boy am I bored. They have the prettiest red mud around camp. However we went for a route march this morning and the mud was the usual colour farther away from camp. Yesterday afternoon we had the afternoon off & since the tide was out we walked out the shore for about a mile. Then it started to come in so we walked back in. Some excitement eh?…Brother, to think that I might spend 8 weeks or more here. Boy oh boy am I disgusted.*

When Jack transferred to the United Kingdom, he wrote two letters expressing his appreciation of the new surroundings.

April 1944: *Well here I am I didn't get seasick although I wasn't feeling well for a while. Boy oh boy, now I see why the RAF fellows wanted to get home. We saw some of the country, the grass is a lovely green, everything is in bloom … Nothing but the best for us here. We have swell quarters etc. so we are perfectly happy. I wish I could have seen you before I left but maybe it is just as well. You know how I am at saying goodbye … Right now the sun is out and I want to go for a walk.*
May 1944: *I had a wonderful leave. I*

was up at Windermere in the Lake District. Boy it is beautiful country up there it reminds me a lot of Muskoka district in Canada. I spent my leave lounging around, rowing, riding a bike, fishing etc. The fellow where I was staying owns 3 small lakes which he stocks with rainbow trout, speckled trout etc. Boy that's fishing.

The day following the invasion of Normandy Jack wrote:

7 June 1944: *The invasion starts & I am not even on course yet. Most of us are mad because we are starting to wonder if we will see action or not. I wonder? Personally, knowing what we*

> "This English beer is horrible the fellows all want to give it back to the horses. However we can't complain. Well I still haven't seen the inside of a plane over here but I might sometime I hope"

still have to go through, I doubt it … This English beer is horrible the fellows all want to give it back to the horses. However we can't complain. Well I still haven't seen the inside of a plane over here but I might sometime I hope.
16 July 1944: *Well here we are again. About those flying bombs, don't worry we never see them. We are on a beautiful station now. The hut I'm in is about 2 miles from water, except what's in the mud, but then you can't wash in that can you. We have a swell crew here Pilot — Joe Talocka (Polish origin), Nav. yours truly, Bomber Chuck (oh hell I never can remember his last name), Wag — John Davis, Air Gunner Al (Major) Bradley, and "Nookie" Chisamore. As far as flying goes, don't worry, we are the best crew*

around (so we claim). Seriously, the pilot is an F/O who has been flying for quite a while & knows everybody's job. He's better in some parts of nav. than I am. They told me that I am an above average nav. (Please quit laughing, I'm serious) Chuck is an F/O too. The Wag and A.Gs are sergeants.

The fledgling crew continued training, although there were some changes.

3 August 1944: *What a life. I moved barracks the other day & am now sleeping in a single room with a bureau, table, chair etc. Some class I'd say …We had a change in our crew. We lost Chuck our Bomb Aimer & got Arlotte from Toronto.*
21 August 1944: *We lost our WAG today. He was put on charge for smoking on parade & so we will have to get another fellow. He was damn good too.*
17 September 1944: *By the way we could use some canned fruit etc. now that you have a can opener. Please note that I said we. Whenever anyone in the crew gets a parcel the whole crew gangs up on him & there goes another parcel. But we all have fun anyway. I wish you could meet the crew. They are a swell bunch. Joe (the pilot) is a real gen boy. You can't catch him on the questions on flying. He lands these big crates as if he were carrying eggs …We have been looking forward to this leave for quite a while and it promises to be quite a blow out. And how. Our little mid upper doesn't drink so he will keep us in hand. I sure wish I could see you again soon. Maybe I will be able to. This war can't last long.*
28 September 1944: *Then we came here, our new station. I have just finished fighting for two hours with the fire in my room to get it to burn. Then I gave up. What a place. A second Maitland. However it won't be too bad. We won't be flying for about a month again so you can breathe easy for that long anyway… Edie sent me some hot chocolate & oxo in hers but we have no place to make it so I*

had to give most of it away to the batwoman. We haven't got any here. What a life.

On 2 October 1944 Jack wrote to his sister telling her of some of the sights he had seen on leave. It was not going to be something he wrote home to his mother about.

All you can do in this country is go out & get drunk. I had a leave last week in London & had quite a time. You walk along the street dodging the Piccadilly commandos (Eng. type of lower class of Montreal so&so girl). Boy are they thick around there. They charge anything from £2 (9 bucks) to £5 (about $22.50) Some girls. You should see some of them.

As the nights lengthened and the war entered a sixth winter, Jack kept his mum posted of his frustrations and further details of his crew.

8 October 1944: *Well here is your son Flying Officer Styles writing again (that sounds nice doesn't it). Still disgusted with your homeland. What a country. As far as heating goes they haven't got a clue. They stick a little stove in a huge room & everyone freezes. Then when they have a very small room they stick a huge stove in it & everyone sweats. Boy oh boy they haven't got a clue. Back at school again …Always in school.*

12 November 1944: *Did I tell you about our engineer, he is an English fellow, and very keen. He knows the Halifax inside out …His name is Graham Needham, I am going to give you his number soon, when I get it, & you can try to send him cigs. By the way, I haven't got any cigs for quite a while now. Try to send a thousand next time will you?*

1 December 1944: *Well I finally have some pictures for you. They are pictures taken in Manchester and a couple here. I am sending a few now and some copies of the ones from Manchester later so that you*

Left: 'Our crew'.
Below left: Joseph Chisamore.
Below right: Joe Talocka.
Below centre: Jack Styles and 'Red' MacLean.
Bottom: Sidney Arlotte, Jack Styles and Joe Talocka.

Right: A picture of the crew dated 12 January 1945.

can send some to Norma & Grandma.

There is one very good one of the whole crew, all sober etc. The one of Red and myself is pretty good. Red is another Nav. that I know. He is getting married over here soon.

In Manchester there were only five of us and we took the pictures. So most of the pictures only have five of us in them (sensible isn't it).

By the way, if you notice a queer look on my face don't blame me. I was trying to smile through a hangover or something. Some fun. I like the picture of Joe with the whole crew rather than his alone. It looks more like him. Chis of course looks very serious, don't let it fool you he usually isn't so serious …They are a swell bunch.

18 December 1944: This is quite a place. At last we are out of Nissen huts. In fact it is swell.

3 January 1945: Well here it is 1945, & still a war on. Oh well maybe it will stop soon. At last I can try to do my bit instead of doing nothing.

12 January 1945: Don't get too much of a surprise, I know that I haven't written for a week but I was on leave, you know, a holiday. We had a swell leave, went to Glasgow (in Scotland you know). …That was my first trip to Scotland & it was swell. The people are swell.

I went up with our mid-upper "Brad" who also went to see his friends …We spent a very quiet leave, I only had 3 (THREE) pints (or maybe four but no more) in a week, but we still had fun. "Brad" doesn't need any drinks, he is crazy enough as it is.

…I'm glad you liked the snaps. I was afraid you wouldn't get them. You like the crew eh, so do I, hope you can meet them sometime, they are a swell bunch of fellows. By the way Joe's number for the interested parties is J35641 F/O J.P. Talocka & he says that he will answer all fan mail personally. Seriously if you or anyone else write him for heavens sake no mush …

You wish I could be home by summer, so do I. Keep your fingers crossed and for heavens sake try not to be too lonely. I want you to be happy …Your loving son, Jack.

At the end of January 1945 Jack and his crew took part in a large raid in the Stuttgart area and on the night of 1/2 February Jack's was one of 340 navigators entrusted with directing his crew to Mainz. The following night Bomber Command sent 323

Right: The RAF Manston log recording the fate of Jack Styles and five of his crew.

| 3.2.45. | DAY. | Halifax of 426 Squadron, which crashed last night is located, but there are |
| | | no further survivors. |

aircraft to attack the oil refinery at Wanne-Eickel, which proved ineffective due to difficulties with cloud cover. Owing to the extensive damage to Jack Styles's Halifax, Joe Talocka had tried to land at RAF Manston. The station diary recorded, 'A Halifax of 426 Squadron crashed while making wide circuit with controls shot away. All attempts by Police, NFS, and our own ambulance parties to find aircraft fail. One survivor who bales out thinks the aircraft crashed in Minster Marshes. 11 Group lay on land and sea search for this aircraft.' The following day the diary recorded, 'Halifax of 426 Squadron, which crashed last night is located, but there are no further survivors.' ∎

Canadians Joe Talocka, Joseph Chisamore, Sidney Arlotte, Allan Bradley, and Jack Styles were all buried at Brookwood Military Cemetery. Graham Needham was taken back to his home town and buried at Scunthorpe (Brumby and Frodingham) Cemetery.

Left: The four graves of, from left to right, Allan Bradley, Joseph Chisamore, Sidney Arlotte, and Jack Styles, at Brookwood Military Cemetery.

JACK MORRIS STYLES

Nationality: Canadian
Rank: Flying Officer (Nav.)
Unit: 426 Squadron
Service No: J/42042
Date of Death: 03/02/1945
Age: 20
Son of Reuel Clarence Styles and Jessie Styles, of Arnprior, Ontario, Canada.
Grave/Memorial Reference: 56. G. 1.
Cemetery: Brookwood Military Cemetery

Far left: Jack Styles.
Middle left: The headstone of Jack Styles at Brookwood Military Cemetery.
Left: The headstone of Joe Talocka, in the same row as his crew mates.

Unless stated otherwise all pictures are 'Used with the permission of the Styles family and The Canadian Letters and Images Project'
http://www.canadianletters.ca

Many thanks to Dr Stephen Davies, Project Director at The Canadian Letters and Images Project, and to George Lord.

Brookwood is 30 miles from London (M3 to Bagshot and then A322). The main entrance to Brookwood Military Cemetery, the largest Commonwealth war cemetery in the United Kingdom, is on the A324 from the village of Pirbright. There is a direct train service from Waterloo to Brookwood Station from which there is an entrance to the cemetery. For further details see the Commonwealth War Graves Commission website **http://www.cwgc.org**

Hurricane over the Adriatic

The airmen of No. 6 Squadron Royal Air Force, had already demonstrated their ground-attack capabilities in the North African campaigns. The title of the squadron newsletter, *The Tin Opener* hinted at what they had been doing to enemy tanks in the desert. Then in 1944 came a change. The squadron moved to Italy, with the pilots flying Hurricane IVs armed with rocket projectiles. Their task was to find, harass, and destroy the shipping being used by the enemy in the Adriatic Sea, particularly amongst the islands off the Yugoslavian coast, with the odd incursion inland to attack enemy camps and transport. The support to the partisans, who were fighting to expel the Germans from their country, was invaluable.

24 July 1944 – A Hawker Hurricane Mark IV of No. 6 Squadron RAF being serviced on an airfield in Italy, probably Foggia Main, prior to a sortie over the Adriatic.

IMAGE IWM CNA 3035

Freddie Nicoll through the years...

Right: At ITW in Torquay, 1941.
Centre: May 1942.
Far right: Whilst with No. 208 Squadron – winter 1942/3.
Bottom right: At his home, February 2009.

FREDDIE NICOLL

selection, his aspirations came under scrutiny. 'I had had a good education and considered myself a bit of a bright lad. I thought a pilot was the thing to be.' But one of the interviewers queried why Freddie did not want to be an air gunner, stating, 'You think the air gunners all come back shot-up, dead.' Freddie replied 'Oh no', keeping his inner thoughts to himself. 'People knew the air gunners were vulnerable, especially in the old planes they operated in. Anybody who flew those things deserved a medal straight away in my opinion.'

'Above average'

Freddie's future lay in the cockpit of an aircraft, starting his air force career at No. 3 Initial Training Wing in Torquay. From here he went to Liverpool, then by Sea to Cape Town where he was entrained for Rhodesia (Zimbabwe). 'After three weeks in a troopship the journey from Cape Town to Bulawayo was sheer luxury. There was a buffet car. Our bunks were made up for us with clean sheets. Whenever the train halted at a township the platform was lined with tables laden with fruit, cakes and drinks, served by smiling ladies. It was on 5 November that we were at last entrained (third class) from Bulawayo to Salisbury (Harare) to commence our flying training. It was on this journey that I celebrated my twenty-first birthday with a tin of pears!'

Freddie set about learning the art of flying at No. 28 EFTS Mount Hampden and No. 22 SFTS Thornhill. He gained his first 'Air Experience' on 10 November 1941: a 50-minute flight in a Tiger Moth.

At one point in his training an instructor told Freddie that he really had to concentrate more on his aerobatics if he wanted to be a fighter pilot. When Freddie told him he did

Whilst growing up in Walthamstow, north London, Freddie Nicoll occasionally marvelled at the spectacle of Alan Cobham's Flying Circus, 'You could see some of the aerobatics going on from my back yard.' Then in 1940 he had gazed skywards watching the aerobatics of airmen in battle. 'I witnessed a lot of the planes coming over during the Battle of Britain and I saw a lot of the bombing that

"After three weeks in a troopship the journey from Cape Town to Bulawayo was sheer luxury. There was a buffet car. Our bunks were made up for us with clean sheets. Whenever the train halted at a township the platform was lined with tables laden with fruit, cakes and drinks, served by smiling ladies"

went on in London. I was quite concerned about what was happening, a worrying time – the idea of invasion.' Another aspect of the struggle against Nazi aggression also focused Freddie's mind. 'I didn't like the idea of the ships being sunk, with children on them, and the food that was needed for this country. I thought I would join the air force and fancied myself touring over the Atlantic and destroying submarines.'

Freddie signed up for the Royal Air Force, and was called up in May 1941. At final interview, prior to

not want to fly fighters the instructor appeared mortified. Freddie still held a yearning to hunt for submarines in multi-engined aircraft. Nevertheless Freddie performed well during training, achieving 'above average' assessments, and in July 1942 he was sent to No. 74 Operational Training Unit at Rayak in Syria. Previously, when he had received his Wings, he had been earmarked as a reconnaissance pilot, a role he would develop whilst flying Hurricanes at No. 74 OTU, although his first solo in a Hurricane had not gone too well.

I made a heavy landing. I was very nervous. I was on my own and had no previous experience. The Hurricanes were very old, Mark Is. It didn't take too much of a heavy landing to cause damage. If you did the drill was to open up the throttles and go round again, which I did. Then when I selected to put the wheels down I only got one green light. You would get two green lights to show that they were locked and down, so I knew something was wrong. I came in and made what I thought was a perfect wheels landing. I thought this was the proper thing to do. As I lost speed the damaged undercarriage gave way, with a little turn at the end, damaging the wing tip and propeller tip. That was all the damage.

An ambulance come out to greet and rescue me, with a very keen young medical chappy standing on the running board. When he got near the Hurricane he leapt off and the fellow broke his leg. He went back in the ambulance, whereas I went back with the tractor.

Tactical reconnaissance

Having completed his tactical reconnaissance training Freddie was posted to No. 208 Squadron in North Africa arriving on 13 September 1942 and the following day carried out some local flying practice in a Hurricane II (Z3357). For the rest of the month he built up the hours, notably 'Formation Evasive Tactics Weaving', and on 3 October carried out his first operation 'Escort to Dawn Sortie', 'Weaver to P/O Bezencenet. No ack-ack. Southern Front'.

FREDDIE NICOLL

FREDDIE NICOLL

Freddie played an active role in No. 208 Squadron's Army co-operation and reconnaissance duties, taking part in some of the reconnaissance duties prior to the opening of the Second Battle of El Alamein in October 1942. On one occasion, having been involved in a sweep of the whole front line, which was supported by a formation of Hurricanes from another squadron, Freddie had a bit of a scare as he came in to land. 'We were always trained to look in our rear mirror and when I did I saw this other Hurricane, the last of the formation, swoop down on me. It transpired he was a new member of his squadron. Having seen a lot of dust on the ground, and an aircraft with wheels down, he had assumed it was a German Stuka, which had a fixed undercarriage. I guessed he was coming after me so I rapidly got my wheels up and got out of the way.' Freddie did eventually receive an apology from the CO of the Hurricane squadron, which had been carrying out the support cover.

As it was, Freddie was not with No. 208 Squadron long before it was rested, 'The ground crews were exhausted', and they were sent back to Syria and then Iraq. Over the course of the next year the squadron would carry out Army co-operation training, including some uneventful patrols whilst in Iraq. Then following a spell in hospital, fighting malaria, Freddie was posted to No. 6 Squadron, a unit he had certainly heard about: 'They were the famous tank-busters.' Freddie joined up with the squadron at Fayed on 9 October 1943, and two days later carried out 'Rocket Projectile Practice' in a Hurricane IV. On that same day the squadron diary recorded, 'In view of the squadron's impending move to an operational sphere, all pets such as dogs and cats are being disposed of either by destruction or by giving them to personnel in other units who have permission to accept them.' However, on 15 October news came through that 'the Squadron will not at present be required for operations. A telephone call from Group Captain G.T. Carrill-Worsley of H.Q., R.A.F., M.E., instructed that pilots of this squadron are now to be trained in low level bombing. Three aircraft are to be fitted with bomb racks and a suitable target located by the Commanding Officer preferably in a deep wadi. Training is to commence immediately.'

Through November, December, and in to the New Year, further ground-attack practice was carried out, including the occasional 'Tank Beat-up'. At the beginning of April 1944 Freddie and his No. 6 Squadron colleagues found themselves in Italy, 'Much to our horror when we got there they said you are not going to be on anti-tanks, you are going to be anti-shipping.'

STEVE DARLOW

On 16 April 1944, operating from Grottaglie, Freddie Nicoll took part in an attack against the enemy with three colleagues.

Aircraft	Pilot	Details	Time up	Time down
Hurricane IV KX.178 P	F/L R.H.C. Powling	Attack on hutted camp	15.33	17.28
Hurricane IV KZ.187 X	F/O C.B. Black	ALBANIA		
Hurricane IV LB.683 Y	F/O F.J. Lawrenson (RAAF)			
Hurricane IV KX.402 Z	F/O F.J. Nicoll			

4 aircraft detailed to attack enemy M.T. and Camp area in ALBANIA in area 39.56N, 20.16E. Aircraft armed with 4 x 60lb HE. SAP. RP and 1 x 45 gallon long-range tank. Attack in conjunction with 4 Spitfires of 249 Sqdn. Aircraft airborne 15.33 hrs and flew on course 115 degs. And then 90 degs. to arrive at target area 16.35 hrs. 6/8 MET seen on main road which runs due WEST to EAST from coast. At 39.56N. 20.16E Hutted Camp attacked, which consisted of 4 large, rectangular wooden block huts approx. 100–120 ft. long, together with 3/4 stone buildings in camp area. Hurricanes dived from 5,500 ft. to 1,500 ft. releasing rockets in dive. All salvoes were seen to strike in camp area starting one fire with a considerable quantity of black smoke. After the attack the aircraft flew to the coast and returned to base on a course 295 degs. The MET on main road reported above was identified as 1 large vehicle and 5–6 smaller 15 cwt. Type trucks, travelling WEST spaced 100–150 yards apart. Vehicles halted as aircraft flew over and troops baled out of rearmost vehicles and made for cover. The Spitfires attended to this target and also 4 MET on the same road EAST of "T" junction. Visibility excellent over target area. No movement seen on coast road N. to S. No flak encountered during operation. No E/A seen.

No. 6 Squadron met with considerable success during April 1944. Claims for the month were recorded in the squadron diary as follows:

Destroyed/Sunk		Damaged	
5 Barges	3 Schooners	8 Barges	1 Railway engine
3 Siebel Ferries	1 1,500 ton vessel	2 Siebel ferries	2 Landing craft
1 "F" Boat	(3-island type)	4 Schooners	4 schooners
1 2,000 ton cargo vessel	5 other vessels	1 x 1,000 ton coaster	1 "F" boat
1 A.C.V.	3 Landing craft	1 x 3,000 ton tanker	2 Radar Stations
1 Radar Station	1 Gun position	7 Other vessels	2 Radar Stations
	1 Radar Mast	2 Marking Lights	1 3-ton M.T. truck
		1 Glass Marker Buoy	1 Railway Stn
		1 Lighthouse	1 Railway tunnel entrance
		1 Railway engine	1 Railway station roof
		3 Railway trucks	2 Railway petrol trucks

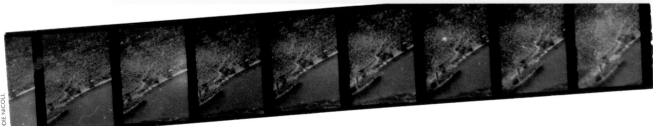

FREDDIE NICOLL

Based at Grottaglie, near Taranto, in the heel of Italy, Freddie and his colleagues began their offensive sorties across the Adriatic Sea. 'In order to extend our range so that the whole of the Adriatic could be covered a forward base was established on the island of Vis.' Although Freddie's first visit to the island was somewhat unplanned. The day, 3 May 1944, was also marred with the loss of one of the squadron's pilots – Captain Leisegang. Freddie made out a written report.

FREDDIE NICOLL

I was flying No. 2 to Captain Leisegang who was leading an attack by four Hurricanes in the vicinity of Ploca (43° 04'N, 17° 26'E). The target was four schooners in a creek. I followed Captain Leisegang through heavy flak to the target at ground level about 300 yards behind him. I saw him fire his rockets, but did not observe the results, as I had turned to attack another schooner. On leaving the target area at approx. 10:45, Captain Leisegang called up on the R/T saying his aircraft had been hit in the radiator. I then observed his aircraft flying south at 1000', with a stream of white smoke coming from it; I was on his port beam at 0' and about 800 yards away. As I endeavoured to close with him, he called up again saying he was wounded in the leg, and then again saying he could not see. There was a lot of

noise on the R/T but when I was about 200 yards behind him I heard him say, "Hurry up, hurry up! My speed is down to 120." As we were then over the sea at approximately 42° 52'N, 17° 24'E and at 2000'I told him to bale out. Just as I got level he half-rolled and baled out. I saw the chute open, saw Captain Leisegang strike the water, saw the dinghy inflate and the chute drift away. I then began to climb over the spot and tried to contact "Fruity" and "Topsail" [Vis]. This was difficult because many people were speaking on the R/T. At 10,000'I contacted "Topsail" who gave me my bearing from Vis as 095°. I continued to circle at this height. The dinghy was invisible, but the patch of oil left by the aircraft was plainly visible. As I was getting short of petrol, the Controller at Vis vectored me to the island, saying that the A.S.R. launch was on its way out. I landed about 11:30, and was taken to the controller. I told him Captain Leisegang had baled out in the Mejetski Channel; but he thought it was in the Nevetljanski Channel, and had sent out the launch on a course of 090°. He had also asked Spitfires from Foggia to escort the launch. As the islands were obscured by low cloud, I thought it best to accept his judgement. Owing to difficulties in refuelling I was not able to take off again until 16:00 hours, when I searched the whole of the Mejetski Channel together with two Spitfires of 32 Squadron. We found no trace of the dinghy, but I saw the oily patch of water at the Western end of the

Channel, which was confirmed by one of the Spitfire pilots. All further search was then abandoned.

F O F.J.N. 'B' Flight. No. 6 Sqdn

Freddie returned to the island of Vis following the search for Captain Leisegang, where he had to spend the night.

I spent the night sleeping in a kind of shepherd's hut. They gave me a couple of blankets which were covered in fleas, it was a most uncomfortable night. I went back to the mainland the next day where my ground crew were pleased to see me. I did have a narrow escape because one bullet had actually gone through my aircraft and missed the main fuel supply by a few inches. It could have been disastrous.

South African Lieutenant (Pilot) C.G. Leisegang, 22 years old, is buried in Belgrade War Cemetery.

Left: Preparing for a trip to Cairo. Freddie Nicoll, standing on the far right, and Leisegang at the bottom left, early 1944.

Through May operations continued. On 23 May Freddie recorded in his logbook: '16. ATTACKED LARGE TANKER – CHERSO HARBOUR. DIRECT HIT WITH SALVO. (PARTISANS REPORT SHIP "SUNK").' Here is Freddie's recollections of the day, followed by the official account.

There were six of us on detachment on *Vis*, one of whom was my flight commander. He sent four out that morning to attack some shipping up in the north but only two of them came back, unfortunately. We knew one of them came down. In the

Spitfires could see down. So we climbed and looked down and lo and behold at the end of a stretch of water was the harbour, with a big tanker moored, and with a big swastika on it. It was the first time I had really seen a boat with a huge swastika. So I thought, 'Oh, this is it!' Robin called up to me and said, 'This is worth a posthumous DFC', and we both went in to attack. I saw his rockets fall short and go along the water, but I was able to get a direct hit on the side of the tanker. The flak followed us on the way out.

Later the Partisans said that it had sunk, but I didn't think

"One of the Spitfire pilots called up and said, 'There's a bloody big ship in a harbour down there.' My flight commander, Robin Langdon-Davies, a very laid back character, said, 'We'll go and have a look'"

afternoon he and I set off with an escort of four Spitfires, which gave us top cover so we could concentrate on what was going on down below and not worry about what may be above. We couldn't find any trace of this unfortunate character.

One of the Spitfire pilots called up and said, 'There's a bloody big ship in a harbour down there.' My flight commander, Robin Langdon-Davies, a very laid back character, said, 'We'll go and have a look'. We were flying at low level and we couldn't see over the rising ground of the island on our left, whereas the

it had. I think it was put out of action. I went to Navy Headquarters in Taranto and identified the ship. Apparently it wasn't used for carrying fuel, it was used for transporting fresh water to German garrisons all the way down the Croatian coast. Naturally the Germans didn't trust the wells because the Partisans had a nasty habit of poisoning them when they weren't looking. They managed to tow the tanker back to the mainland but it was never in use again, so it was as good as sunk as far as I was concerned. Quite a day really!

Right: No. 6 Squadron prior to the move to Italy. Freddie Nicoll is back row second from the left.

FREDDIE NICOLL

On 23 May 1944 the squadron diary recorded the following:

Pilot	Details	Time
S/Ldr J. H. Brown DFC, F/Lt R.H. Langdon-Davies, F/O P.B. Stewart, F/O J.N. Grey, F/O F. J. Nicoll, P/O W. Tye (NZ)	Flew to VIS and refuelled awaiting target.	06.30

11.15 4 Hurricanes accompanied by 2 Spitfires of No. 253 Squadron were airborne to carry out a recce of PODGORSKI CHANNEL. No movement seen but later S/Ldr Brown sighted an armed schooner. He machine-gunned and was followed by P/O Tye who fired RPs from 50–100 yds. His salvo striking amidships and blowing away superstructure and mast. He called up and said his engine was running roughly and he was told to return to VIS. Nothing further was heard from him and he did not arrive at VIS. F/O Stewart and F/O Grey then attacked with unobserved results. F/O Grey called up to say his aircraft was damaged, S/LDR Brown then attacked with R.P. and blew away the stern of the ship which sank. On the way back P/O Grey reported that his engine was cutting and he was told to bale out. He baled out clear of his aircraft but his parachute did not open until just before he hit the water. The remaining two pilots circled but there seemed to be no chance for his survival.

14.30 F/Lt R.H. Langdon-Davies and F/O F.J. Nicoll with 2 Spitfires of No. 253 Sqdn. Carried out an armed recce and search for the two pilots missing from the previous operation. The area was searched without result. Continuing on offensive recce a large ship 2–3,000 tons was seen in CHERSO Harbour and both pilots attacked, a direct salvo hit being obtained causing a considerable explosion. Target left in heavy pall of black smoke. Continuing a small motor vessel was seen and attacked with M.G. by Hurricanes and with M.G. and cannon by Spitfires. Target was left stationary.

Casualties: P/O W. Tye (NZ.411957) and F/O J.N. Grey (125837) Missing.

Both 22-year-old John Grey and 24-year-old New Zealander William Tye are commemorated on the Malta Memorial.

Keeping up the pressure

Through June, July, August, and into September, Freddie Nicoll and his No. 6 Squadron colleagues maintained a continual presence harassing the enemy shipping, most of Freddie's operational flying carried out from Vis. It did not go all their way; there were losses including the CO Squadron Leader 'Jasper Brown'. Freddie comments on the build-up of the stress and pressure over the summer months.

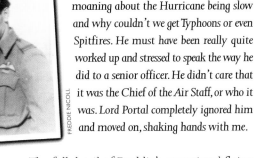

Without realising it I think a lot of us were getting quite washed up. There was no such thing as counselling in those days. One time the squadron was inspected by Lord Portal, who was then Chief of Air Staff. He came out to Italy to inspect all the air force squadrons. We knew he was coming to our squadron and we all lined up. Along came Lord Portal with other high ranking officers, wearing khaki shorts exposing white knobbly knees, shaking hands with the pilots and chatting as he went along. As he got nearer to us I heard him say, 'What a wonderful aircraft the Hurricane is. Every year we find a new use for it.' And when he got to my friend standing next to me he said, 'Don't you agree?' 'No Sir!' he snapped at him. He had always been moaning about the Hurricane being slow and why couldn't we get Typhoons or even Spitfires. He must have been really quite worked up and stressed to speak the way he did to a senior officer. He didn't care that it was the Chief of the Air Staff, or who it was. Lord Portal completely ignored him and moved on, shaking hands with me.

The full detail of Freddie's operational flying during the period, as recorded in his logbook, is shown on the following pages 104–7.

Left: Squadron Leader James Brown DSO, DFC, killed on 27 August 1944, age 27. Commemorated on panel 12, column 2 of the Malta Memorial.

CHAPTER EIGHTEEN

Below and right: Cargo vessels, May 1944.

Far right: Picture of a 'wrecked schooner' taken on 3 June 1944. A typical target for Freddie Nicoll and his colleagues.

FREDDIE NICOLL'S LOGBOOK – NO. 6 SQUADRON OPERATIONAL SORTIES				
DATE – 1944	AIRCRAFT		DUTY	TIME
2 APRIL	HURRICANE IV	LB649	ARMED RECCE – CORFU	1.55
13 APRIL	HURRICANE IV	KZ402	ATTACK CORFU HARBOUR	1.45
14 APRIL	HURRICANE IV	LB683	DO. ABORTIVE SORTIE	1.10
15 APRIL	HURRICANE IV	LB683	ANTI-SUB PATROL	1.45
16 APRIL	HURRICANE IV	KZ402	DIVE ATTACK – HUN CAMP	1.50
17 APRIL	HURRICANE IV	LB683	ANTI-SUB PATROL	1.30
17 APRIL	HURRICANE IV	KZ321	ANTI-SUB PATROL	1.30
23 APRIL	HURRICANE IV	KZ402	ARMED RECCE CORFU	1.50
3 MAY	HURRICANE IV	LB649	ATTACK SCHOONERS – PLOCA	1.30
3 MAY	HURRICANE IV	LB649	SEARCH FOR DINGHY	1.00
6 MAY	HURRICANE IV	KX876	SUBMARINE PATROL	1.35
13 MAY	HURRICANE IV	LB649	OPS, AT FIER RADAR STN	1.45
15 MAY	HURRICANE IV	LB649	ATTACK RADAR – CORFU	1.45
16 MAY	HURRICANE IV	LB649	ATTACK COASTAL STEAMER	1.50
20 MAY	HURRICANE IV	LB649	ATTACK E-BOAT OFF CORFU	2.05
23 MAY	HURRICANE IV	LB649	SEARCH FOR 2 PILOTS AND RECCE	2.15
24 MAY	HURRICANE IV	LB649	A.S.R. SEARCH	1.00
27 MAY	HURRICANE IV	LB649	ARMED RECC. N. SHIPPING CHANNELS	2.25
			ATTACK M/V LUSSIN	1.40
29 MAY	HURRICANE IV	LB649	ARMED RECCE. N. CHANNELS	1.45
31 MAY	HURRICANE IV	KX178	ARMED RECCE	1.50
1 JUNE	HURRICANE IV	LB649	ATTACKED GUNS ON BRAC ISLAND	.40
7 JUNE	HURRICANE IV	LB649	DAWN RECCE	1.50
10 JUNE	HURRICANE IV	LB649	DAWN RECCE	2.05
			MORNING RECCE	2.15
12 JUNE	HURRICANE IV	KZ243	MORNING RECCE	2.20
24 JUNE	HURRICANE IV	LB649	LAST LIGHT RECCE	2.15
			DAWN RECCE	2.15
1 JULY	HURRICANE IV	LB649	NIGHT OPS. LAND PESCARA	2.20

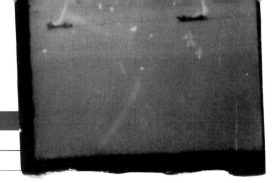

DETAILS

1. NO SHIPPING SEEN

2. DIVED ON SMALL SHIP IN HARBOUR (2 BANDITS)

3. RETURNED OWING TO BAD VIS.

4. ADRIATIC. NOTHING SEEN

5. LEFT FIRE (OIL – REFUELLING POINT)

6. NOTHING SEEN

7. DO.

8. RADAR STATION ATTKD. NOTHING ELSE SEEN

9. SALVOE HIT SCHOONER. INTENSE FLAK. 'JEEP' BALED OUT

10. FROM VIS WITH TWO SPITS. SAW PATCH OF OIL

11. ADRIATIC

12. NO MASTS VISIBLE. FLAK. FIRED SALVOE ON GUN POSNS.
    MACHINE-GUNNED RADAR STN. CAPE GACIL

13. SALVOE IN AREA OF MAST. LIGHT FLAK

14. IN CREEK. DIRECT HIT WITH SALVOE. NO FLAK (1500 TONS?)

15. NO SIGHTING. BELIEVED SUNK BY SPITS EARLIER

16. ATTACKED LARGE TANKER – CHERSO HARBOUR. DIRECT HIT WITH
    SALVO (PARTISANS REPORT SHIP "SUNK")

17. NOTHING SEEN. RETURNED TO VIS

18. NO SIGHTINGS AT SEA ATTACKED ? 2000 TON M/V LUSSIN PICCOLO.
    MODERATE FLAK. DAMAGED SHIP

19. SAME M/V DIRECT HIT WITH SALVO.
    LEFT LISTING + BURNING. FOLLOWED OUT BY FLAK

20. NO SUITABLE TARGET SEEN. R.P.'S LEFT AT VIS

21. SECTION ATTACKED 120' SCHOONER – NEAR MISS WITH SALVO
    LIGHT FLAK. (OTHER SECTION – 2 SIEBEL FERRIES) LUSSIN PICCOLO

22. ATTACKED SUPETAR HARBOUR. FIRE STARTED. 20mm FLAK

23. M/V LEAVING LUSSIN PICCOLO 500/1000 TONS. HEAVY FLAK. WRECKED. SALVO
    PROBABLE UNDER WATER LINE

24. ATTACKED 2 SCHOONERS RAB. CREW GOT ASHORE. VERY DIFFICULT TO GET AT

25. SCHOONERS IN CHERSO. 1 SUNK 2 DAMAGED (LATER CONFIRMED AS SUNK)
    20mm FLAK

26. ATTACKED SCHOONER & BARGES – CHERSON BAY. NO HITS. EXTREMELY ROUGH AIR

27. FLAK FROM LUSSIN P. SANK 80' SCHOONER WITH SINGLE. 1 SCH.
    SAN PIETRO 2 SCH OLIB DAMAGED

28. 2 INACTIVE F BOATS N. OF KORCULA. WRECKED ONE WITH SALVO.
    FLEW THROUGH INTENSE FLAK ALONG PELJESACKI CHANNEL

29. CHANNELS & ISLANDS SWEPT SAW NOTHING

FREDDIE NICOLL – LOGBOOK SUMMARY CONTINUED FROM PREVIOUS PAGE...				
DATE – 1944	AIRCRAFT		DUTY	TIME
3 JULY	HURRICANE IV	LB649	NIGHT OPS. LAND PESCARA	2.20
7 JULY	HURRICANE IV	LB649	NIGHT OPS. LAND PESCARA	2.25
15 JULY	HURRICANE IV	KZ397	OPS? DESTROYER IN CHERSO	2.20
21 JULY	HURRICANE IV	LD169	OPS	2.20
27 JULY	HURRICANE IV	KZ224	OPS. ITALIAN COAST	2.20
30 JULY	HURRICANE IV	LB649	OPS. PO ESTUARY	1.40
2 AUGUST	HURRICANE IV	LB649	OPS. ARM'D RECCE N. ADRIATIC	2.15
3 AUGUST	HURRICANE IV	LB649	NIGHT OPS	1.50
4 AUGUST	HURRICANE IV	LB649	OPS	2.05
7 AUGUST	HURRICANE IV	KZ726	OPS	1.40
13 AUGUST	HURRICANE IV	KX881	OPS	2.15
15 AUGUST	HURRICANE IV	LB649	OPS. LANDED BIFERNO (NO BRAKE PRESSURE)	2.30 2.30
1 SEPTEMBER	HURRICANE IV	KZ726	NIGHT RECCE	2.10
5 SEPTEMBER	HURRICANE IV	KZ905	ARMD RECCE	1.50
7 SEPTEMBER	HURRICANE IV	KZ905	ATTACK SHIPPING N. HVAR	.45
8 SEPTEMBER	HURRICANE IV	KZ915	PATROL CHANNELS AROUND HVAR	1.40
8 SEPTEMBER	HURRICANE IV	KZ394	DAWN RECCE	.40
10 SEPTEMBER	HURRICANE IV	KX821	ARMD RECCE – TO RAB	2.15
10 SEPTEMBER	HURRICANE IV	LB774	ROAD RECCE KNIN – BIHAC	1.40
11 SEPTEMBER	HURRICANE IV	KX821	ANTI-SHIPPING PATROL – ZARA – RAB.	2.10
13 SEPTEMBER	HURRICANE IV	KX881	DAWN PATROL KORCULA – SPLIT – ZARA	2.10
14 SEPTEMBER	HURRICANE IV	KZ905	DITTO	2.10
25 SEPTEMBER	HURRICANE IV	KZ905	OPS. ALBANIA	2.00
30 SEPTEMBER	HURRICANE IV	KZ905	OPS. DROP MAPS at IST. RECCE	2.10
1 OCTOBER	HURRICANE IV	KZ575	OPS. ARMD RECCE TO RAB	2.00
1 OCTOBER	HURRICANE IV	KZ575	OPS. COASTAL GUNS – PLOCA (NAVY SHELLED HARBOUR)	1.05
4 OCTOBER	HURRICANE IV	KZ575	OPS. ATTACK NIN JETTY	2.10
5 OCTOBER	HURRICANE IV	KZ575	OPS. SARANDE (ALBANIA) AREA	2.00
7 OCTOBER	HURRICANE IV	KZ575	OPS. ROAD CONVOY ALBANIA	2.00

30. S/L BROWN ATTACKED BARGE & SCHOONER SAILING TO CHERSO. MADE SEVERAL ATTEMPTS, BUT DID NOT FIRE. FLAK FROM VESSELS & FROM OWN ACK-ACK

31. PODGORSKI & PLANINSKI CHANNELS. BELIEVED DAMAGED BARGE AT SOUTHERN END

32. CHERSO – NOTHING SEEN. ATTACKED 60/80' BARGE IN SENJ. SALVO HIT – LEFT BURNING. FLAK FROM PRIVLAKA & ZARA ON RETURN HOME

33. DAMAGED BARGE, TWO SCHOONERS ON STOCKS AT ALEXANDROVO. SMALL SCHOONERS IN KRK SUNK

34. REACHED RIMINI. RETURNED OWING TO CLOUD

35. DAMAGED DREDGER, BARGE, & RIVER BOAT (25LB R.P.)

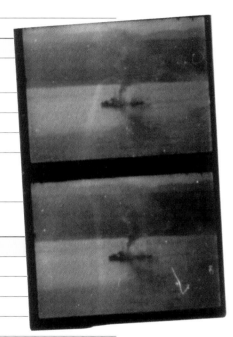

36. SCHOONER SUNK AT ARSA CHANNEL. 1 DAMAGED FURTHER N. AT FIANONA. TWO DESTROYED AT NOVI (Jettisoned L.R. Tank – hit)

37. MISSED SMALL SCHOONER. DAMAGED SIEBEL F. WITH 3 25LB R.P.

38. SWEEP FOR F/LT WALKER. SANK SCHOONER & METAL BARGE

39. STEAMER REPORTED GUANARO. NOT SEEN. DESTROYED 60–80' SCHOONER ISTRIA

40. TWO SIEBEL FERRIES JABLANAC. 1 R.P. STEEP DIVE ? NEAR MISS. 2 R.Ps IN COLLECTION OF BARGERS – PRIVLAKA – 4 OR 5 SUNK. (Ground sources later confirmed 1 Siebel blew up. Also Siebel concealed in barges destroyed)

41. ATTACKED SCHOONERS IN PAG BAY. NO FLAK. (Ground sources confirmed 4 destroyed) (1 Sank with 2–25lb R.P.)

42. SWEPT NORTHERN DALMATION CHANNELS. SAW NOTHING

43. DESTROYED 2 BARGES PRIVLAKA & PAG HARBOUR

44. MUCH FLAK. ONE 'I' BOAT SUNK. OTHERS DAMAGED

45. NOTHING AT SEA. 20mm E. HVAR (So close heard guns firing!)

46. INTERCEPTED CONVOY N.E. HVAR. INTENSE FLAK. ONE F BOAT IN FLAMES. ONE CLAIMED DAMAGED

Above: Cargo vessel, May 1944.

47. BLEW UP TWO SIEBELS IN RAB HARBOUR (P.R.U. state 2 A.L.C.'s. Ammo. Oil dump and 45' launch destroyed. Smoke up to 3000')

48. ATTACKED CONVOY WITH 4 SPITS. CLAIMED 5 LORRIES DEST

49. ATTACKED 500 Ton M/V S. PAG. LEFT BURNING – NO SUPERSRTUCTURE (When 4 a/c went to finish it off, there was smoke & flames 6ft high)

50. NOTHING ATTACKED. REPTD PILES OF BOXES – TJESNO

51. STRAFFED 30' BOAT NEAR PLOCA. SET STORES ON FIRE AT TJESNO. SWING BRIDGE ALSO ATTACKED

52. GUN PITS, ROAD BRIDGE & WOOD – ATTACKED BY 5 A/C. N. OF SARANDE. NO FLAK

53. ATTACKED IN CREEK S. JABLANAC. 1 SIEBEL OR A.L.C. LEFT SMOKING. 1 SIEBEL POSSIBLY HIT

54. NOTHING SEEN AT RAB. STRAFFED LOPAR HARBOUR. SECTION ATTACKED GUN POSITIONS S. OF BIOGRAD

55. STRIKES IN GIVEN AREA – DIVED FROM 8000'. SCANT LIGHT FLAK

56. SCORED NEAR MISS ON FLAK SCHOONER. BRIDGE DAMAGED. STRAFFED RADAR STATION – LUSSIN. DROPPED MESSAGE AT IST. MOD. FLAK. NIN

57. VERY BAD WEATHER. ATTACKED GUN SITE NISOS – CORFU. FIRE STARTED – AMMO. BLEW UP (Third attack; finished off position)

58. ATTACKED 30 PLUS VEHICLES NEAR ELBASAN. MANY HIT AND DAMAGED. SCANT LIGHT FLAK

One noticeable entry in Freddie's logbook concerns the attack on two Siebel ferries in Rab Harbour on 10 September 1944. Freddie recently wrote a short account of the action.

On 10 September 1944 I found myself leading a formation of four rocket-firing Mk IV Hurricanes on an armed reconnaissance over the Adriatic, operating from our forward base on the island of Vis. The object was to look for any stray shipping, attack and, if possible, sink it!

Prior to take-off we were informed by Intelligence that Partisan sources had reported the presence of two Siebel Ferries in the harbour at Rab, a small island towards the north of the Adriatic. (A Siebel Ferry was a large ocean-going barge capable of carrying troops or any kind of cargo, used extensively by the Germans.)

We carried out a wide sweep for about an hour at 5,000 feet and saw nothing! So I ordered the formation to get in line-astern, adding "let's go and have a look at Rab".

When we were down to about 1,000 feet I noticed flak coming from a small island just off Rab, so I called up to warn them to start weaving. It was at this point I realised my radio had decided to pack up! We skimmed over the elongated harbour at low-level, and there, moored along one side and quite close to each other, were the two Siebels! Normally I would have called up the formation to switch on their wing-mounted cameras and switch off the rocket safety catches — but no radio!

I climbed to gain a little height, executed a 270° turn to port, came in over the trees and then over the roof-tops, with a

Right: A picture taken by Squadron Leader Paish of No. 208 Squadron captures Freddie Nicoll leading a section of 4 Hurricanes on armed reconnaissance to Rab, 10 September 1944.

Siebel Ferry in my sights. Out of the corner of my eye I caught a glimpse of a man running along the quayside — his feet appearing not to be touching the ground. I grinned to myself, and prayed he would get away in time! I fired my salvo of four rockets, each with a 60lb H.E. head, and immediately broke right. This manoeuvre was essential to avoid flying into one's own explosion.

I then turned to look back and saw a Hurricane with its wings silhouetted against a huge orange ball of flame. I thought his number was up — but was wrong. It emerged with the whole fuselage holed like a pepper-pot but engine running. It transpired later that No. 1 target had been laden with diesel fuel, which accounted for the thick black smoke rising to 10,000 feet and No. 2 target had been laden with ammunition. No wonder that poor fellow was running away like hell!

By some miracle or fluke my radio came alive again, and my No. 2, the pilot of the damaged plane, informed that we was OK apart from having no flying instruments working, including no airspeed indicator. We steered a direct course across the open sea to Vis, where a successful formation landing was made on the airstrip, which had been constructed among the island's vineyards.

But the story does not end there. By sheer coincidence, while the raid was going on, a pilot from P.R.U. flying a Lightning was overhead taking routine photographs of all the harbours, which enable Navy H.Q. to plot the movements of enemy shipping. I was able to meet him at a later date. He was Squadron Leader Jack Paish, and we had known each other in 1942 while both serving in the Middle East with No. 208 Squadron.

The attack by the No. 6 Squadron Hurricanes did indeed cause considerable damage. Further photographs taken by Squadron Leader Paish would show substantial amounts of smoke billowing from the harbour.

My logbook states 'Blew up two Siebels in Rab Harbour'. The P.R.U. reports states 'Two A.L.C.s — Ammunition dump, oil dump and 45 foot launch destroyed. Smoke up to 3,000 feet.' Duration of flight: 2 hours 15 minutes.

Later in the day, escorted by four Spitfires, we attacked a road convoy between Knin and Bihac and claimed five lorries destroyed. Duration of flight: 1 hour 40 minutes.

I can't remember much about the second trip, but the visit to Rab (now a deservedly attractive resort for yachtsmen and walkers) is certainly engraved on my mind.

Early in October 1944, with the details of 58 No. 6 Squadron operational sorties inscribed in his logbook, a decision was made to rest Freddie Nicoll, against his wishes. He had asked his friend Robin Langdon-Davies, who was then the CO, if he could stay on but was told, 'You take my advice and go home, marry that girlfriend of yours and have lots of little Nicolls.' Freddie arrived back in the UK to take up duties at No. 51 OTU in January 1945, then a short spell on Typhoons at No. 55 OTU in April, prior to spending six months at No. 4 Delivery Flight, and finally with No. 631 Squadron on Army co-operation duties on the Welsh coast, from October 1945 to May 1946.

Freddie's flying days with No. 6 Squadron had earned him a Distinguished Flying Cross. A letter from 'Air Headquarters "X"' summed up the appreciation of his abilities, 'I should like to thank you for the grand and very gallant work which you did whilst in 242 Group. You more than earned your DFC – thank you.' ■

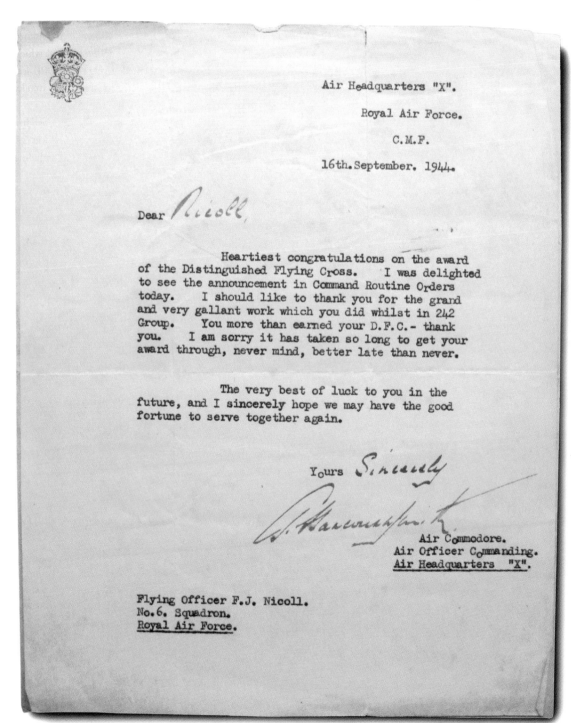

Air Headquarters "X".

Royal Air Force.

C.M.F.

16th. September. 1944.

Dear Nicoll,

Heartiest congratulations on the award of the Distinguished Flying Cross. I was delighted to see the announcement in Command Routine Orders today. I should like to thank you for the grand and very gallant work which you did whilst in 242 Group. You more than earned your D.F.C. – thank you. I am sorry it has taken so long to get your award through, never mind, better late than never.

The very best of luck to you in the future, and I sincerely hope we may have the good fortune to serve together again.

Yours Sincerely

Air Commodore.
Air Officer Commanding.
Air Headquarters "X".

Flying Officer F.J. Nicoll.
No. 6. Squadron.
Royal Air Force.

Left and below:
Freddie Nicoll's Distinguished Flying Cross and the letter from 'Air Headquarters "X"' congratulating him on the award.

Wood Where the Bombers Came Down

The gathering of friendly bombers – it was a sight that enthralled and captivated many civilians during the war. The glint of metal and the roar of hundreds of engines lifted many an eye skywards, to witness United States Eighth Air Force four-engine bombers assemble into formation prior to setting course for hostile airspace. It was certainly a spectacle but there were occasions when those on the ground would witness terrible tragedy. One such occasion occurred in August 1944, and a recent event rekindled the memory of that dreadful day.

On the morning of 26 August 2007, a small group of people made their way to a wood near a small village in Hertfordshire, England. They were there to commemorate an incident that had taken place sixty-three years earlier and resulted in the loss of life of 14 American airmen and 2 civilians. In the party were Mark and Howard Bettinson, the nephew and brother-in-law respectively of one of the airmen who lost his life. Also in attendance was aviation archaeologist Julian Evan-Hart. This would be a moving day for Julian; he had been investigating the incident they were commemorating most of his life:

In the early 1970s I first heard people in the village of Weston talking about the 'Wood where the bombers came down'. I was only about 10 years old and I cycled over to Warrens Green and parked my bike next to a hollow area used by local gardeners to dump old vegetable cuttings and large stones. By pure chance I was just looking around when I spotted a large bullet with a brown coloured patina, just lying on some recently deposited earth. Picking up this 'treasured item' I examined it closely noting that it had probably detonated in the fire caused by the exploding bomber. (Little did I realise then that 35 years later I would be in the same area looking at the ground, this time finding an exploded 0.50 calibre shell case, but this time would be extra special as I would be in the company of the relatives of one of the aircrew.) The fact that my bullet had hit something at very high speed was clearly evident by its now flattened tip, which should have been pointed. I remember thinking that it looked like the snub wrinkled nose of a pig!!

B17G FLYING FORTRESS (UNNAMED)
Serial Number: 42-102936
390th Bombardment Group (Heavy)
Based at: Parham/Framlingham in Suffolk
Location: Wreckage spread over 1.5km in Weston Park

CREW

Pilot: 2nd Lt Paul H. Bellamy		Killed
Co-pilot: 2nd Lt James J.Graba		Killed
Navigator: 2nd Lt Raymond A. Klausing		Survived
Bombardier: 1st Lt Joseph Y. Lee		Killed
Radio Operator: Sgt Irwin W. Casey		Killed
Eng/Top Turret Gunner:		
S/Sgt Frederick O. Walsh		Survived
Waist Gunner: Sgt Lotus R. Conser		Survived
Ball Turret Gunner: Sgt Robert Hunter		Killed
Tail Gunner: Sgt Richard A. McAteer		Survived

B17G FLYING FORTRESS NAMED 'DING DONG DADDY'
Serial Number: 42-97182
390th Bombardment Group (Heavy)
Based at: Parham/Framlingham in Suffolk
Location: In Warrens Spring Wood at Weston

CREW:

Pilot: 1st Lt George E. Smith		Killed
Co-pilot: 2nd Lt Carleton Sacco		Killed
Navigator: 2nd Lt Robert G. Taylor		Killed
Bombardier: 2nd Lt Herman R. Collins		Killed
Radio Operator: T/Sgt Victor G. Graff		Killed
Eng/Top Turret Gunner:		
T/Sgt Allen J. McCasland Jr		Killed
Waist Gunner: S/Sgt Martin I. Kilbride		Killed
Ball Turret Gunner: S/Sgt Michael K. Kasarda		Killed
Tail Gunner: Corporal Gus G. Brubaker		Killed

Main image, opposite: A somewhat over-exposed yet evocative photograph of some of the crew sitting on the wing of 'Ding Dong Daddy'.

Left: Robert G. Taylor (right) navigator of 'Ding Dong Daddy' and co-pilot Carleton Sacco. Both men would lose their lives in the collision.

Left: Mark Bettinson (right) holds a piece of 'Ding Dong Daddy' with Julian Evan-Hart.

Thus began a 37-year interest in the crash site. Over the years Julian made numerous visits to the site, discovering the collision involved two B-17 Flying Fortresses, finding bomb craters; uncovering small contorted pieces of metal, bits of rubber and wires; a layer of compressed and burned parachute fabric, in amongst which were some harness clips and a complete 'D Ring' still attached to a 6-inch length of thin wire; cockpit instrument faces; electrical bits; airframe; a pair of headphone receivers; jack plugs; wiring; switches. Julian has pieced together an account of the collision, which he published in his book *War – Torn Skies of Great Britain - Hertfordshire*.

Whilst researching the incident for his book Julian made contact with some relatives of the crew, and just before his book went to press he was contacted by Mark Bettinson, the nephew of the navigator of 'Ding Dong Daddy' Robert G. Taylor. Mark shared the details he had with

and then we heard other noises, Mum and Dad thought it was a German plane up with the others and a Spitfire after it, as we could hear tracer bullets going off when the explosion went off. Mum said 'good they must have shot that Jerry down' but how wrong we were. It was the two B-17s colliding and coming down.

At the time we lived at the Rising Sun Public House at Halls Green, and my father had just made a cup of tea for us, my brother David was still asleep. My father ran down the stairs and went outside to see what was wrong as I ran out after him I asked him 'what was all that coming down in the sky?' I remember seeing all the black smoke coming up from Warrens Green Woods, and all the debris coming down, also an airman without a chute and another one coming down and his chute was burning, what a terrible thing to see. The sky was full of pieces of all shapes and sizes falling and the sun shone on it and everything seemed to twinkle. I can remember a Fire Tender pulling up after a while and they asked my Father if he could tell them where to go. My Father said 'I'll just put my jacket on and come and show you the way'. We did not see him for the rest

> "I remember seeing all the black smoke coming up from Warrens Green Woods, and all the debris coming down, also an airman without a chute and another one coming down and his chute was burning, what a terrible thing to see"

Julian and expressed a wish to come to England and visit the scene of his uncle's fateful accident. And so it was that in August 2007 Mark and his father-in-law Howard flew across the Atlantic to meet Julian.

A visit to the scene was scheduled for the actual anniversary day, but before that, Mark and Howard visited the crash site and met a lady by the name of Alice Cherry, who had witnessed the incident, and now owned the land where the B-17s fell to earth. Mark and Howard also made a visit to the RAF Museum at Hendon, went to see the remains of the station at Framlingham, from where 'Ding Dong Daddy' had taken off, and then attended a family wedding in Norfolk.

'That day was going to be different...'
Meanwhile, on 24 August 2007 Julian received a letter from Mrs Ruth Wainwright who lived in Stevenage, a few miles from Weston. Part of this letter is quoted below:

I remember the 26 August 1944, very well, although only eight and a half years old. Mum was expecting a baby in October 1944 and as it was a Saturday she said we could all have a 'lay in bed' until the postman came at 9am. But that day was going to be different and the postman would not come! We could hear the B-17s all going over

of the day; at about 7.30pm he came home, but did not talk about what he had been helping with and what he saw, only to say he helped comfort the Clements family [who had lost two members of their family when the wreckage came to earth] and helped out at the Anchor Public House. He said it was all too sad to talk about and a dreadful thing to have happened; and he did not talk about it ever!!! I went out over the meadows with a friend and found a yellow rubber like case with a gun and bullets in it. I was told later it was a pistol for Verey lights, I wanted to keep it, but my friend must have told her father and the next I knew was a Policeman and an ARP Warden coming to my house and asking me what I had found!! After some talking I showed them the case and said 'I want to keep it' but they said it must be handed over. I got upset about this and still said I wanted to keep it as I had found it!! I was told no way could I keep it and the family would be in trouble if we kept it, so I handed it over!! I also came upon a petrol tank in a field and a lot of the silver paper as we called it that the planes carried. For a few weeks the Bomb Disposal Unit was in the area also looking for unexploded bombs etc etc!!

Stirring memories
So it was that on Sunday 26 August 2007, the sixty-third anniversary of the collision, the relatives of one of the men lost, some eye witnesses to the incident, and Julian

Left: A dollar bill sent home by Robert Taylor including signatures of some of the crew – Carleton Sacco (far left), George Smith (just left of centre), and Herman Collins (written vertically above the left 'N' of the serial number).

Evan-Hart, whose research had stirred the memories, assembled to pay their respects. Julian recounts the day:

I was up by 0700hrs and awaited the arrival of everyone at our agreed time of 0800hrs outside my house. People began to arrive from just past 0800hrs, finally followed by Mark and Howard who had driven all the way back from Norfolk this morning. We set off in convoy and met Alice Cherry at the site, as well as Mrs Ruth Wainwright [who wrote the letter above] and her two sons. She was introduced to Mark and Howard and told them what she had seen 63 years ago. The weather was absolutely perfect with blue skies and fleeting high-level clouds; Mrs Wainwright said this was exactly as it had been on the 26 August 1944. Interestingly she said that the day back then started as such but by late afternoon it was drizzling. Jason Baker, a friend and Chairman of the Fenland Finders Metal Detecting Club, had also brought along four medium-sized firework rockets to mark the event. Timing had to be precise and at 0900hrs Mark and Howard were positioned in the woodland at the exact spot where the B17s cockpit had impacted.

Out of respect they were left alone and at 0903hrs they were told this was the exact time of the collision; in four minutes' time at 0907 they were signalled that was probably the time that 'Ding Dong Daddy' crashed into the wood on the very same spot they were now standing on exactly 63 years before. Mrs Wainwright had brought along a bag of red rose petals and she scattered these on the site of the cockpit impact point. After this time photography was tactfully permitted as they came back through the woodland. Bradley my son had been setting up the launching tube for the rockets and we all proceeded round the side of the wood. When we arrived at the northern end of the wood I read aloud the names of the two crews (both those killed and the survivors) and also the names of the two civilians who had been killed. As soon as I had completed this, on an otherwise windless day, a pronounced breeze sprung up from nowhere, lasted about ten seconds and vanished as quickly as it came. Jason and

Left: Mark and Howard Bettinson at the exact spot where Robert Taylor was killed 63 years earlier.

Bradley then lit and fired off all four rockets. Each one rose high over the green woodland canopy leaving a thin white smoke trail and then terminated with a multicoloured chrysanthemum-shaped airburst and a loud explosion which echoed all over the park. One of the dead rockets actually impacted back to earth about 50 feet away, sticking out of the soil!! It was now that Jason presented Mark and Howard with the polished section of aluminium found a few days before. It had now been fashioned into a key-ring with all the details engraved upon it. Words can never adequately describe pure emotions, but Mark's look said it all. A small piece of 'Ding Dong Daddy' would finally be heading back home again over the Atlantic ocean after some 63 years.

Youthful spirits

We returned back to the woodland and in addition to the unusual breeze that had occurred minutes before, something else began to happen. For some reason this has always been a quiet area, in the thirty years I have spent here I have never heard a bird sing here ever, until now that is. Firstly one bird began to call and was followed by others, robins, woodpigeons, warblers and sparrows were now all singing until the end of the wood seemed to be crammed with bird-song. Now I am not a religious person at all, but something happened here in this wood this morning, perhaps restless angry youthful spirits so prematurely taken away have at last been laid to a peaceful rest …I don't know, but everyone felt it. I know this woodland will never feel the same again; true it is a sad place and always will be when one remembers what took place here, but it will be different now a heavy soulful pressure seems to have been lifted from the area, and perhaps, just perhaps the birds could sense this …again I just don't know. All I know is that whatever did occur here this morning it was good and meaningful. Both Mark and Howard now have a form of closure on an event just a few months ago they knew little to nothing about, and here they were thousands of miles from home in the middle of a Hertfordshire wood. At about 1220 we finally left the wood. Mrs Wainwright and her sons departed, wishing our guests well and hoping they had found peace within themselves. We chatted briefly by the cars and then departed back to my house where, picking up my sons Bertie and Gus, we departed again after several minutes. Our final destination was the Rising Sun Public House where Mrs Wainwright had been born 71 years before. It is still a pub today so we sat in the garden and sampled some local brews. As my two young sons played around, I watched them as they came over to Mark and Howard and watched the reactions of all concerned, different generations, different nationalities all brought together due to the supreme sacrifice made by fourteen American airmen and two civilians nearly seven decades ago; but one young 21-year-old airman was most responsible today for bringing about this remarkable situation over the last few days and this was Second Lieutenant Robert G. Taylor. ■

Right: Howard Bettinson (left) and Mark Bettinson examine a piece of wreckage outside the wood where 'Ding Dong Daddy' fell.

Clockwise from top: Pieces of wreckage found in the area where 'Ding Dong Daddy' fell. Section of parachute; part of throttle quadrant; instrument face; part of VHS radio; burnt penny.

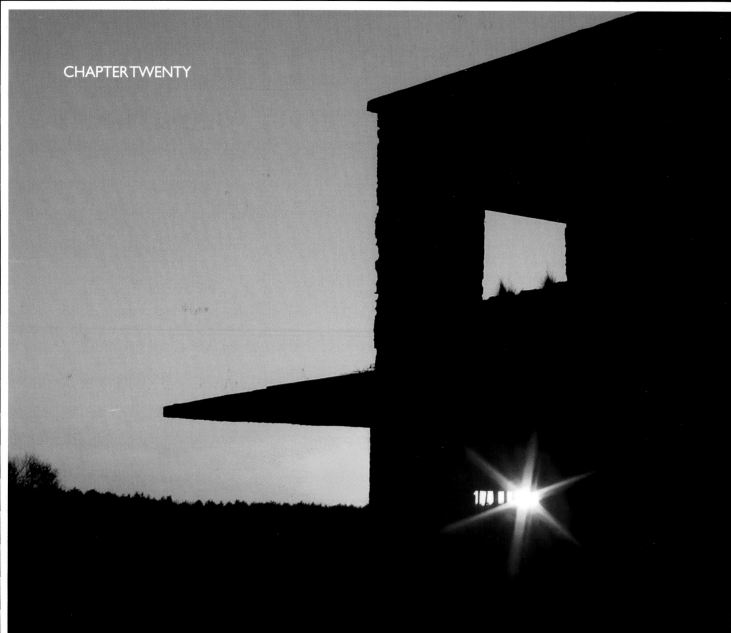

First Light at Little Snoring Throughout the United Kingdom, relics of the air war stand derelict, but many of those buildings not demolished have been put to use. Large hangars contain farming equipment, and weathered watch towers provide storage for farmers, or even act as platforms for clay pigeon shooting. My research into the activities of RAF Bomber Command brought to my attention the airfield at Little Snoring, Norfolk, England. There were buildings still remaining, notably the watch tower. I was fortunate that the land-owner was kind enough to grant access to the private airfield. So early one morning I set off, in the dark, with a view to experiencing daybreak amidst the relics of a Bomber Command airfield.

CHAPTER TWENTY

I had come here to experience first light and cast my mind back to when the airfield was home to airmen of the Royal Air Force's Bomber Command. It was a still and very cold December morning, the sky black, the stars bright. Yet above a line of trees to the east the sky was changing, from black through shades of blue, blending to orange and then yellow, with isolated red-flecked clouds. There was hardly a sound, and a delicate wind cut a slight chill through gaps in my clothing. The ground was whitened with a slight frost, which had hardened the mud sufficiently to allow passage across the field of stubble, and not hinder footfall. Standing sentry-like and proud, in the middle of the airfield was an old watch tower; the window frames now rusted and bent; the walls weathered and the interior floors gritty. Large boxes, high in the rooms, provided shelter for the current inhabitants, barn owls.

As I stood in the field of stubble looking at the watch tower husk, with the sun yet to show, I began to think back on what it must have been like waiting for bombers to return from the east all those years ago. Then the activity as the Lancasters or Mosquitoes came into land; returning from long flights through hostile airspace, with tired crew, who still had to relate their experiences. Some aircraft may have had casualties on board. And at some point someone would have to officially declare some of the bombers as having 'failed to return'.

On this cold winter morning, at first light, I tried to capture the atmosphere on my camera. I also took time to remember those who gave their lives flying from Little Snoring airfield.

On the night of 20/21 October 1943, No. 115 Squadron's Flight Lieutenant John Anderson took off from Little Snoring with his crew, totalling eight, detailed to take part in an attack on Leipzig. The Lancaster failed to return, the entire crew buried in Berlin 1939–1945 War Cemetery.

On the night of 18/19 October 1943 21-year-old Sergeant Sidney Allen of the Royal Canadian Air Force was killed during a night fighter attack over Hannover. Two other members of the crew were injured. Despite the considerable damage to the No. 115 Squadron Lancaster, two engines out and elevators and trimming control shredded, the pilot, Warrant Officer E. H. Boutilier RCAF, wrestled the bomber back to Little Snoring. An immediate Distinguished Flying Cross recognised Boutilier's skill, along with a Distinguished Flying Medal for one of the injured airmen – Sergeant Rogers. On return to Little Snoring Sergeant Allen's body was taken from the aircraft, to be subsequently interred at Cambridge City Cemetery. On the same night Sergeant John Whitehead's crew of seven would not be returning, all now resting in the Reichswald Forest War Cemetery.

CHAPTER TWENTY

i General information

The airfield, a few miles north-east of Fakenham, Norfolk and lying to the east of the road between Little and Great Snoring, hosted a number of operational Bomber Command units during World War Two. First to move in was No. 115 Squadron in August 1943, with Lancaster IIs (along with No. 1678 Heavy Conversion Unit, which only stayed a few weeks). When the airfield was re-designated as a home for No. 100 (Bomber Support) Group, No. 115 Squadron departed and in December 1943 the Mosquitoes of No. 169 Squadron arrived, followed by the Beaufighters of No. 515 Squadron (which were soon to be replaced by Mosquitoes). No. 169 Squadron left in June 1944 and No. 23 Squadron moved in.

The RAF Bomber Command website www.raf.mod.uk/bombercommand/s24.html) records 55 Bomber Command aircraft lost in operations flying from Little Snoring: 12 Lancasters and 43 Mosquitoes.

On the night of 18/19 March 1945, whilst over Belgium, the No. 515 Squadron Mosquito, piloted by 24–year–old Flight Lieutenant Arthur Hirons DFC, and navigated by 21–year–old Flight Sergeant Peter Williams, collided with a No. 425 Squadron Halifax. Hirons, Williams, and six of the crew of seven on board the Halifax lost their lives, and all now rest at Hotton War Cemetery.

Twenty-year-old Pilot Officer Raymond Peate of the Royal Australian Air Force lost his life with his entire No. 115 Squadron crew, when they were shot from the night sky by a German night fighter during the 18/19 November 1943 raid to Berlin. The crew of eight now rest in Heverlee War Cemetery.

Flying Officer Frank Byrne of the Royal Canadian Air Force (in fact an American from Phoenixville, Pennsylvania) lifted his No. 515 Squadron Mosquito from the Little Snoring runway at 2340 hours on the night of 12 May 1944, setting course for Twente. The cause of the loss was never established, the North Sea only prepared to relinquish the body of navigator Sergeant Victor Payne, subsequently interred at Sage War Cemetery. Byrne is commemorated on the Runnymede Memorial.

CHAPTER TWENTY

Early on the afternoon of 13 February 1944 23-year-old Flight Lieutenant Peter Bowen of No. 169 Squadron lifted his Mosquito II from the runway at Little Snoring, to carry out a training flight. Less than half an hour later the aircraft plunged into the sea a few miles off Burnham, Norfolk. Bowen's body was never found and he is commemorated on the Runnymede Memorial. His navigator, 35-year-old Pilot Officer John Atkinson, who came from Leça da Palmeira in Portugal, rests in Cambridge City Cemetery.

Early on 2 April 1945 Squadron Leader Penny of No. 515 Squadron witnessed a ground explosion whilst on a sortie to Leipheim airfield. Initially he believed Lieutenant Emile van Heerden of the South African Air Force, flying another of the squadron's Mosquitoes, had claimed an enemy aircraft. But Heerden and his RAF navigator, Flying Officer James Robson, would not be returning to Little Snoring. Both men rest in Dürnbach War Cemetery.

ACKNOWLEDGEMENTS

SOURCES

In addition to the people already mentioned at the end of chapters, our thanks extend to Chris Thomas, Chris Goss, Pete West, John Davies (Grub Street), Mark Postlethwaite, Steve Teasdale, Declan O'Flanagan, Steve Fraser, Rob Thornley, Steve Kitchener, Michael Lindley and Mark Etherington for their help and support.

Most of the material published in Fighting High is based upon primary sources. However the following secondary sources have also been consulted.

Crook, D. *Spitfire Pilot* (Greenhill Books, 2006)

Darlow, S. *Lancaster Down!* (Grub Street, 2000)

Chorley, W.R. *RAF Bomber Command Losses of the Second World War – 1943* (Midland Publishing, 1996)

Chorley, W.R. *RAF Bomber Command Losses of the Second World War – 1944* (Midland Publishing, 1997)

Chorley, W.R. *RAF Bomber Command Losses of the Second World War – 1945* (Midland Publishing, 2004)

Evan-Hart, J. *War-Torn Skies Hertfordshire* (Red Kite, 2007)

Marshall, B. *Angels, Bulldogs and Dragons: The 355th Fighter Group in World War II* (Champlin Fighter Museum Pr, 1985)

Middlebrook, M. and Everitt, C. *The Bomber Command War Diaries: An Operational Reference Book, 1939-45* (Midland Publishing, 1998)

Shores, C. *Those Other Eagles: A Tribute to the British, Commonwealth and Free European Fighter Pilots Who Claimed Between Two and Four Victories in Aerial Combat, 1939 – 1982* (Grub Street, 2004)

Shores, C. and Williams, C. *Aces High: A Tribute to the Most Notable Fighter Pilots of the British and Commonwealth Forces in WWII* (Grub Street, 1994)

INDEX

Page numbers in italics indicate illustrations.

INDEX

STEVE DARLOW